Beyond the Food Court

Beyond the Food Court

An Anthology
of
Literary Cuisines:

Essays

Edited by
Luciana Erregue-Sacchi

LABERINTO PRESS

Copyright © 2020 by The Authors
Introduction copyright © 2020 by Luciana Erregue-Sacchi

Except for purposes of review, no part of this book may be reproduced in any form without permission of the publisher.

We acknowledge:
the support of the Edmonton Arts Council for our publishing venture.

Cover and book design by Matthew James Weigel

Library and Archives Canada Cataloguing in Publication

Beyond the Food Court, An Anthology of Literary Cuisines (2020)
  Beyond the Food Court, An Anthology of Literary Cuisines: Essays
    Edited by Luciana Erregue-Sacchi
    Concept Editor: Yasser Abdellatif

Issued in print and electronic formats.
ISBN 978-1-7770859-0-2

1. Food Court—Canada—Edmonton—Literary essays.
2. World cuisines, Canadian (English).
3. Canadian Literature (English) 21st century.
4. Erregue-Sacchi, Luciana, 1967- Title.

Printed and bound in Canada

LABERINTO PRESS Ltd.
7407 119 Street
Edmonton, AB T6G 1W2
Canada

www.laberintopress.com

"Eating with the fullest pleasure—pleasure, that is, that does not depend on ignorance—is perhaps the profoundest enactment of our connection with the world. In this pleasure we experience our dependence and our gratitude, for we are living in a mystery, from creatures we did not make and powers we cannot comprehend."

—*Wendell Berry*

Contents

Introduction — 8

Culinary Languages

Notes on Dor, Poetry, and Learning to Cook in Quarantine — 14
  Adriana Oniţă (*Romania-Canada*)

Le Hosanane Ke Letatsi: Tomorrow is Another Day — 24
  Peter Midgley (*South Africa*)

Culinary Geographies

Egyptian Cuisine: Historical and Geographical Features — 32
  Yasser Abdellatif (*Egypt*)

Masgouf: The Crown of Iraqi Cuisine — 38
  Maitham Salman (*Iraq*)

Culinary Politics

Disposable Double Double Lives — 44
  Mila Bongco-Philipzig (*Philippines*)

Of Curries and Custard Apples: Identity, Memory, Resistance — 52
  Asma Sayed (*India*)

Biryani, Beef Lynchings, and the Kristallnacht of India — 60
  Tazeen Hasan (*Pakistan*)

Resolviendo — 68
  Ana Ruiz Aguirre (*Cuba*)

Culinary Heritage

Five Recipes   76
    Anna Marie Sewell (*Canada*)

Empty Mason Jars   84
    Marco Melfi (*Italy-Canada*)

Culinary Nostalgia

Missing the Beloved Injera   90
    Shimelis Gebremichael (*Ethiopia*)

Food Ties   98
    Leilei Chen (*China*)

Culinary Arts

Sauerkraut Tableau and Other Art Installations   108
    Wendy McGrath (*Canada*)

Pen Portraits with Mate and Asado   114
    Luciana Erregue-Sacchi (*Argentina*)

Introduction

The usual venues where we congregate to eat, drink, and be merry have transformed into something even more sterile than the food court. Due to COVID-19 measures, we have had to adjust—even if only for a few months—to physically distant ways of socializing. I honestly miss heading to the mall, and on a whim, walking about the stalls of ethnic and fast foods, traditionally presented in apparently distinctive ways, according to national identities, while under the sameness of bright logos, plastic cutlery, paper bags, and glistening Styrofoam containers. Missing these trivial excursions has made me examine more closely the different cuisines and their distinctiveness from one another, in the Canadian context. There, waiting to be explored, lies a blind spot bursting with centuries-old tales of maritime travel, economic crises, mutual influences, wars, agricultural practices, displacement, immigration, acculturation, and other human examples of cultural exchange.

    The authors behind this anthology have studied their own hungers, to paraphrase American food writer M.F.K. Fisher. Their vivid re-telling of past culinary experiences bears little resemblance to the—now more than ever—sanitized version of the food court. It becomes a collective exercise of remembering and creating new memories as your eyes settle on the words Masgouf, asado, Injera, or ajiaco. Both food and speech are experienced in the mouth, as Peter Midgley's piece on his family connection to Afrikaans cuisine and Adriana Oniţă's testimony of learning to make maternal Romanian dishes attest. What makes these essays relevant is their Canadian-ness, and I am not referring to an immutable, sterile notion of national identity. Many Canadians speak and write in a second, and sometimes third language, as do some of the contributors. Compiling this anthology satiates our hunger to open up the field of CanLit. The introduction of foreign words, such as in the title of Ana Ruiz Aguirre's piece *Resolviendo*, constitutes a successful instance of literary creation. The Edmonton Arts Council, through the Cultural Diversity in the Arts Grant, has single-handedly legitimized this collective effort of curating and self-publishing this anthology. This endeavour also speaks to the need for driving change in the local publishing world.

    Creative non-fiction is commonly referred to as fact-based writing that uses the techniques of fiction to bring its stories to life. The works in this volume borrow from literary journalism, memoir, and essay, to cultural criticism. Wendy McGrath's *Sauerkraut Tableau and Other Art Installations* draws from the vocabulary of visual culture. Food consistently signals to the borders of what we might term national bodies as in Mila Bongco-Philipzig's text on Filipino migrant food workers as casualties of the COVID-19 pandemic, and the geographical and natural borders behind Arabic cuisine as in Yasser Abdellatif's and Maitham Salman's pieces. These cross-border relationships meld "Domestic" languages with imported new vocabularies alongside new cuisines, as in Leilei Chen's and Shimelis Gebremichael's contributions. Other times the essays expose intolerance towards minorities as in Tazeen Hasan's piece on beef biryani and the prosecution of the Muslim minority in India. Asma Sayed's essay, on the other hand, waxes lyrical on her personal memories of Indian food, and simultaneously probes its diasporic context. These geographic juxtapositions expose the specificity of individual culinary experiences; not one instance of consuming and preparing beef biryani reads the same as another.

The food court as we have known it has become a relic of sorts, in need of re-arranging. The editors have chosen, rather than organizing the pieces according to nationalities, or the ethnicities of the writers, to organically connect the works, moving from the geographical aspects of culinary experiences, to the intersection between food and geography, politics, heritage, language, and nostalgia. This movement allowed for new connections to be made between the cuisines, the authors, the different nationalities, and the texts themselves.

Please help yourself to the feast unfolding in front of you.

—Luciana Erregue-Sacchi, Edmonton, June 2020

Culinary Languages

Adriana Oniță (*Romania-Canada*)
Notes on Dor, Poetry, and Learning to Cook in Quarantine

Peter Midgley (*South Africa*)
Le Hosanane Ke Letatsi: Tomorrow is Another Day

Adriana Oniţă
Notes on Dor, Poetry, and Learning to Cook in Quarantine

Palermo, Sicilia. Five weeks into quarantine, our souls have melted into dor. All senses and feelings boiled into that one simple word. Dor. Try saying it out loud, taste it, hold its zeamă acrişoară on your tongue. Carry it in your jaw ca o amintire, ca limba română. In English, there are only imperfect synonyms for dor. Longing. Missing. Hankering. Sorrow. Grief. Wish. Woe. They taste a bit off. But I'm not sure what to add for it to taste right. Or what to take away. La fel ca o poezie. Like a poem.

At first, we felt dor as something being taken away from us, hunger from our bodies, light from our souls. Each day we digested a new list of what was closed, what was cancelled, what was prohibited.

> Scuole chiuse. Spettacoli cancellati. Baci vietati.
> Teatri chiusi. Voli cancellati. Abbracci vietati.
> Musei chiusi. Incontri cancellati. Matrimoni vietati.
> Mercati chiusi. Treni cancellati. Funerali vietati.
> Negozi chiusi. Laboratori cancellati. Passeggiate vietate.
> Parchi chiusi. Concerti cancellati. Tutto vietato.

And at first, hearing these words, chiuso, cancellato, vietato, we were fevered with dor for what no longer could be. Our limbs were severed. Our feasts fell through and out of language. How do we acculturate to their absence? Is joy allowed? Can we still touch? How can we hunger? What will we eat? Who will be eaten first?

Italy quickly decided what was essential and non-essential for pandemic survival. Food: essential—dal pane in giù (what could be below bread?). Notebooks, pens, markers: non-essential. Cordoned off at the supermarket. Non sono beni di prima necessità.

New multisyllabic words most of us have never uttered, suddenly burn our palate, hotly reverberate off our tongues, teeth, throat. Quarantena. Ventilatore. Ordinanza. Esponenziale. Then the Covidian words we say quickly then swallow. Contagi. Curva. Colpite. In English, the s sound dominates, sobers, but does not work to soften: Self-isolation. Social-distancing. Unprecedented. Verbs are slimmer, stockpiled for emphasis. Spike. Stock. Flatten. Threaten. Urge. Hoard. Crash. Care. No recipes are offered in any newspaper.

Three weeks into quarantine, dor is capacious. It takes nothing away. O oală mare din ceramică, it is always empty and can only be filled. Dor is clairvoyant, spre trecut și viitor. It reminds us of what we once had, ciò che diamo per scontato. Like my father's Saturday steak, which he has barbecued religiously every week for the last twenty-five years, even in minus forty. Like my mother's ciorbă de perișoare, Romanian sour meatball soup, which I never learned to make in Edmonton because I was running too fast, chasing cada minuto de cada día maximized for productivity. Work—the dor that simultaneously starves and satiates.

In Edmonton, I forgot what food was for. Often, I forgot to eat, let alone cook. I convinced myself there was no time to chop onion, rub leuștean leaves between my thumb and forefinger (and where was leuștean to be found, and how would I translate it, and how do I pronounce "lovage", and how much love is needed?). I lived off drive-thru Tim's bagels, food-court Subways, salami from the Italian Centre, Hello Fresh boxes, and giant Tupperwares of sacred ciorbă de perișoare from my mother—cand mi-era dor, when I found time to drop by for a quick visit, sandwiched between this and that.

My mother arrived in Palermo from Edmonton on a warm February night, a week before the words chiuso, cancellato, vietato were in our repertoire. A week before we were told to flatten our curves (we understood that wrong, took great offense). A week before our souls and organs were starving because all we consumed was news and statistics. A week before nașii mei, my godparents, were to come from Jilava—my uncle's first time on a plane—with their "smuggled" homemade cârnați and telemea on the RyanAir flight. I still taste those smoky sausages and that salty, creamy village feta, forever arriving. Guess I can't have my dor and eat it too.

As I waited for my mother at the Falcone Borsellino airport, I devoured Basilicò, a graphic novel piatto-completo love letter to Palermo by Giulio Macaione, with recipes for caponata, parmigiana di melanzane, cuscus alla trapanese. I couldn't wait to make some of these succulent Sicilian dishes with her. That, and slurp her irresistible ciorbă, that sour soup with borș that I crave mereu, but have never dared to make—despite copying down rețeta into several notebooks.

And as if she could sense exactly what my suflet and body yearned for, my mother made ciorbă the day after arriving in Palermo, this time, with the freshest vegetables from Mercato Ballarò, an ancient open-air market near my new home. Once again, I made sure to jot down her recipe in my notebook, promising her: "Mama, de data asta, o să incerc s-o fac, am timp."

Pentru ciorbă: patru cartofi, două tije de țelină, doi morcovi, o ceapă, un ardei mic, câteva roșii proaspete, sau o cutie de roșii în bulion, carne de pui, călită în puțin ulei să nu facă spumă, Delikat supă de găină, o linguriță de borș pudră, un ou bătut, și pătrunjel, sau frunze de țelină. Vegetalele spălate si curățate se taie in cubulețe de dimensiuni asemănătoare și se pun în oală cu apă rece. Se adaugă carnea de pui puțin călită și bulionul și se fierb 20-30 minute până când vegetalele sunt moi. Ușor. Ai văzut? Spre final se adaugă ingredientul cel mai important: Borșul. După gust. Ție iți place mai acrișoară, nu?

For ciorbă: four potatoes, two celery stalks, two carrots, one onion, one small pepper, a few fresh tomatoes or tomato sauce, chicken meat (fried a little so it won't foam), Delikat chicken soup flavouring, one teaspoon of borș, one egg, and some parsley or celery leaves. After washing and peeling your veggies, cut them into cubes of similar size and put them in a pot with cold water. Add the slightly-fried chicken and the tomato paste and boil it for 20 or 30 min until veggies are soft. Simple, see? Towards the end, add the star ingredient: The borș. To taste. You like it more sour, right?

My mother is Patron Saint of the Kitchen. Sfânta patroană a bucătăriei, făcătoare de minuni. You see—I've never made ciorbă. I've never even made mămăligă. Nor sarmale. Nor chiftele. Nor cozonac. Every woman in my family is extremely pricepută in the kitchen. And me? I can barely boil water. Nu sunt o româncă adevărată, nici nu știu să fac o ciorbă! My mother and aunties remind me that I have other talente, like learning languages, writing poems, being in university for over a decade… And I remind them that none of these things actually feed me. Decât să mă hrănească, they make me starve for a good, wet, hot, sour ciorbiță. That zeamă acrișoară makes me feel like I'm eight again at la Jilava, tugging on șorțul lui Mamaie as she scooped steaming perișoare into a ceramic bowl. My version of Proust's madeleines or Simic's burek. Like Simic, I could write an entire autobiography listing every memorable meal in my life, every dish, every emotion, every story—dar mereu cooked by someone else.

By the time my mother arrived, I had been in Palermo for six weeks with my new husband, and up to that point, I think we only cooked twice. To none of our family's surprise, we had eaten out every day at cheap trattorie. Spaghetti alla Norma from Pastando. The most tender tagliata di manzo, cooked perfectly medio-sangue, from Zangaloro. Mozzarella e prosciutto cotto-stuffed warm pastries from the rosticceria by la Cattedrale. In Sicily, food is the protagonist on every social stage. Food is pleasure. Food is a first kiss, experienced ancora ed ancora. Time is elongated through shopping for ingredients in the thousand-year-old outdoor mercati, savouring a long pranzo in famiglia, or an aperitivo, or a late-night cena with friends. Sicilians and Romanians have that in common—food as an extension of time, an extension of our bodies, melted onto a long table. Food as dor.

When I was nine and what you would now call a newcomer to Edmonton, my family and I would go to the Italian Centre in Little Italy once every few months. It was the only place my mother and I felt closer to acasă—we even found Romanian snacks and mineral water. I remember seeing such delight in my mother's face, enjoying an Eugenie, even if stale, and sipping Borsec water, even if flat, having lost all of its bubbles in the 8,183 kilometres trip to Edmonton. Such unimaginable dor, to taste acasă from afar.

Twenty years later, arm in arm, my mother and I visit Transilvania, a Romanian food store by Palermo's Stazione Centrale. What do we stock up on? We curate a list for survival: mălai, salam de vară, telemea, covrigi, Măgura, Eugenie. "Hai să te învăţ sa faci mămăliga cu smântână, telemea, şi ou," my mother says. She wants to teach me to make comfort food from her youth, for these uncertain times—polenta with sour cream, feta, and fried egg.

A line from Liliana Maria Ursu blossoms: "Acum e februarie şi eu încep să semăn tot mai mult cu mama."[1] I begin to become my mother. This February, deodată, we exchange jokes and folk wisdom with Maria, an elderly moldoveancă who codeswitches română and italiano and recommends vodka for disinfectant. We begin to prepare for an impending lockdown, for a world about to come, and one about to vanish:

Pentru mămăligă: un pahar de mălai la trei pahare de apă, o linguriţă de sare, o lingură de unt. Într-o oală adâncă, (dacă nu, sare în sus şi te arde la degete), se pune apă la fiert împreună cu sarea. Şi încet, sub formă de ploaie, se adaugă mălaiul, care se amestecă în continuu cu o lingură de lemn. Dacă se îngroaşă prea repede, se mai adaugă apă caldă. Aproximativ 30 de minute. Amestecă până când te doare mâna.	For polenta: one cup of cornmeal and four cups of water, one teaspoon of salt. one tablespoon of butter. In a deep pan, (if not, it will jump and burn your fingers) bring water and salt to a boil. And slowly, like rainfall, pour the cornmeal. Stir continuously with a wooden spoon. If it thickens too quickly, add more hot water. Circa 30 minutes. Stir until your hand hurts.

Almost on a desperate whim, we visit il Santuario di Santa Rosalia, the beloved patron saint of Palermo, who is said to have cured the city of the plague. From the winding road up Monte Pellegrino, we see the glory of the city, splayed out between velvet mountains and azure sea.

Santuzza's sanctuary is in a dark, damp cave. We pray for her to protect Palermo, heal our planet.

On our way back, Via Roma is empty. Tutte le strade, deserte. I don't think it hit us until we saw how lonely the streets and piazzas were, how somber the statues in Fontana della Vergogna looked, how slack and open their mouths were, as if to whisper dor for a hundred gazes, lenses, caresses.

And then, the numbers, erect like gravestones. 28 febbraio. 888 casi. 21 morti. 9 marzo. 9,172 casi. 463 morti.

The announcement of national lockdown, nel mezzo della notte. My mother escapes five hours later, on her fifth reissued flight, leaving behind her recipes and dor, and the sweater I still wear as I make my first mămăligă, as a married woman, three weeks into quarantine.

What is food for? What is dor for? In March, all is rain, silence, windows, balconies, grief. Time to think, to feel dor thick in our blood. We have nowhere to rush to. It's an order. "Restate a casa, nelle vostre stanze," the police car blares down our street. Stay at home, in your stanza. Poetry doesn't always have stanzas, but I suppose this is as good a room as any to rest in for a while. Confined. Con fine: with an end. Or, in this case, with no end in sight. Stanza by stanza, room by room, slowly taken over by an invisible foe, like in Cortázar's Casa Tomada.

My brain summons lines of poetry da colazione a cena. "Alone, not less alone than a poem," said Cixous[2]. March 12th, a line by Li-Young Lee awakens me, around noon. "How I wish we didn't hate those years / while we lived them. / Those were days of books, days of silences stacked high."[3] How I wish I didn't hate these days while I lived them. Having spent a decade hoarding words for a full life in my fifth language, how I wish I would have practiced better for silence. Praticare per un silenzio / perforato dalla pioggia.

It's lunch time, March 17th all of a sudden. Ciorbă de pui, the first I've ever made, with fresh bread. I think of our dear Professor Walcott, and all the times we feasted together. Kyoto by Canterra Suites, Elena's in Rodney Bay. It's the day of his death, and I brush my hair, cut my bangs, and video-record myself reciting "Love after Love," first in Italian and then in English, and send it to La Repubblica for their campaign called #c'èbisognodipoesia. The premise—that poetry can save us in pandemic times. Instantly, Patrizia Cavalli's famous line flashes inside my eyelids.

Dinner—mămăligă cu smântână, telemea, și ou. March 22nd, and I recall Derek teaching us how to memorize and recite Auden's "The Fall of Rome," as if we were directors of a great film. I get shivers, the penultimate stanza is on repeat in my head as I bite into yolk: "Unendowed with wealth or pity, / Little birds with scarlet legs, / Sitting on their speckled eggs, / Eye each flu-infected city."[4] March passes, a long stanza of interminable rain. I'm altogether, elsewhere, drenched in dor.

Each day, at 6:00 pm, the breaking news. New numbers appear on the TV screen and they break us, split our lives into prima e dopo. First day of spring: 627 deaths overnight. The next day: 793 souls, gone. As soon as they are announced, they become fiction, uncountable.

By the end of April, Il Sole 24 Ore reports 205,463 casi, 27,967 morti.

Who are the dead? We are not told. What was their last meal? Who did they last speak to? In what tongue? Their coffins accumulate in churches. Their cadaveri—no longer corpi—are dispersed across the country in military convoys. No time for metaphor. Not allowed to lament.

What do we owe the dead? Tenderness. Dor. What do we owe the living? Afternoons with still lives. Evenings with splendidly empty streets. Rallentare, restare a casa, rendere il cuore a se stesso. I think of how poet Ana Blandiana wrote about loneliness—its bare piazzas and clean streets. I witness how singuratatea morphs, through dor, to solidarietà.

Țara arde și baba se piaptănă, is a line I heard a lot in my childhood. The country is on fire, and the old lady is brushing her hair. In times of great chaos, we crave the most regular, mundane things.

In our seventh week in lockdown, I am learning to make orez cu lapte, a comfort breakfast my mother made for me often as a child, over Skype. She eats it with cinnamon powder and I prefer it with cacao powder.

Pentru orez cu lapte: o cană de orez spălat cu apă călduță, un litru de lapte, 2-3 linguri de zahăr după gust, coaje de lămâie sau de portocală. Într-o oală, la foc mijlociu, se adaugă laptele cu zahăr si coaja de lămâie. Apoi orezul spălat. Și amesteci 20-25 de minute. Cacao la sfârșit. Sau scorțișoară.	**For rice pudding:** one cup of rice washed with warm water, one litre of milk, 2-3 spoons of sugar, to taste, lemon or orange zest. In a pan, on medium heat, add the milk, sugar, and lemon zest. then add the rice. And stir. Stir for 20-25 minutes. Finally, add cocoa powder. Or cinnamon.

How futile it feels—learning to feed myself orez cu lapte in a pandemic. How out-of-place is this joy, as I share my kitchen triumphs and blunders with my mother and aunties on video chat. In April, we laugh, 8,615 kilometres apart, at my deformed Easter sarmale, each cabbage roll a wildly different shape and size. "In these viral times, we need to keep our joy contagious,"[5] Edmonton poet Lisa Martin reminds us. Keep our dor alive. Eight weeks into quarantine, many of us would still trade these silent days for the vast afternoon light, a long pranzo in famiglia. Once light returns, may we remember everything we longed for now, and maybe long for this stillness, too. Sper să ne fie dor de poezii, de liniște, de mâncare gătită acasă.

NOTES

1. Ursu, L. M. (2001). În copilărie eram milionară în clipe și secole. *Sus să avem inimile*. Editura Eminescu.
   Reprinted with permission of the author.

2. Copyright 1998 From *Stigmata* by Hélene Cixous.
   Reproduced by permission of Taylor and Francis Group, LLC,
   a division of Informa plc.

3. Li-Young Lee, excerpt from "Braiding" from *Rose*.
   Copyright © 1986 by Li-Young Lee.
   Reprinted with the permission of The Permissions Company, LLC
   on behalf of BOA Editions, Ltd., www.boaeditions.org.

4. "The Fall of Rome," copyright 1947 by W. H. Auden.
   Copyright © renewed 1975 by The Estate of W. H. Auden;
   from *Collected Poems* by W. H. Auden, edited by Edward Mendelson.
   Used by permission of Random House,
   an imprint and division of Penguin Random House LLC.
   All rights reserved.

5. Martin, L. (2020, Mar. 12). COVID-19 a test case in adequate culture and collective behaviour. Gravida and Parity. *Edmonton Journal*.
   Reprinted with permission of the author. https://edmontonjournal.com/life/parenting/gravida-and-parity-covid-19-a-test-case-in-adequate-culture-and-collective-behaviour

Peter Midgley
Le Hosanane Ke Letatsi: Tomorrow is Another Day

    A few years ago, I read an article in which the author asked several noted chefs about their favourite homemade meals. Predictably, some of the more pompous souls among this group of epicureans rattled off creations that sounded more like they'd been whipped up by a top-level sous-chef in an expensive restaurant or on a television show. You know, quick throw-together meals like "Roasted Mascarpone-Filled Dates with Watercress & Brioche." Dinner looks very different for someone who's just shoved the groceries and the kids in through the door after a day's work. But one response sounded real and has stuck with me: a French Michelin chef answered, "Buttered toast."

    Reading that chef's remark brings to mind a story mother would tell us about the time my father, a bank manager, had gone to visit a client who lived on a remote farm. Because of the distance, the client had invited the entire family to stay for the weekend. The hosts prepared a culinary adventure for each meal, but my brother ate nothing. After a day of not touching any of the hosts' food my mother asked for a slice of bread. My brother gobbled it up. And then ate several more. There is something about the smell of butter melting into fresh bread or toast that is wholly satisfying and that can make anyone feel right at home anywhere in the world. As I write this on day something of COVID-19 lockdown in Edmonton, my home for the past two decades, what I long for most is the simplicity of buttered toast.

In desperation, I turned to the familiarity of an old cookbook called *Food for Today and Tomorrow*. The book was originally published during the Second World War to support the war effort, and the compiler is my grandmother, Janet Midgley, who was living in Maseru, Lesotho at that time. Granny Midgley's recipe book always reminds me of my father. Well, one recipe in particular. When he passed away, I flew back to South Africa to spend his last days with him. During a layover in Heathrow, I found a pub that served "Traditional English Fare". I ordered a pint and settled in. One item on the menu stood out: Welsh rarebit. I call it by the name "rarebit" rather than "rabbit" only because that is how it appeared on the menu, and that is what it is called in Granny Midgley's cookbook. Welsh rarebit is a simple dish, but it remains one of the signature recipes from my childhood. And so, in my hour of need in Heathrow I reached for the simple solace I hoped it would provide and indulged in a memory of time I spent with my father as a child.

Once in a while (for cheese was expensive and had to be used sparingly), Dad would pause after listening to the obligatory morning news service on the radio, set down his coffee, riffle through his records and put Beethoven's *Pastoral Symphony* on to play. Then he'd go to the kitchen and start gathering the ingredients—well-matured cheddar, a chug or two of beer or leftover wine, some finely chopped onion, a liberal shake of Worcestershire sauce, and mustard. The result was a pungent goo draped over a slice of hot toast. No fancy accoutrements, just a basic souped-up cheese on toast.

The Heathrow rarebit arrived fully kitted out on two slices of white bread nestled against a bed of baby spinach, with a side of mediocre coleslaw and French fries. The lingering taste of cheap mustard cloyed on my palate like the sound of a bad Amy Winehouse cover. That's when I realized: no chain store generic could ever replace the taste of memory. It simply could not banish the sense of isolation I felt at that moment in an airport transit lounge. What was missing was the taste of Sunday mornings and Beethoven's brook bubbling over a slice of fresh toast.

And so, when COVID-19 started wearing me down, I reached for Granny Midgley's cookbook and the comfort of her Welsh rarebit. It is the taste of "home", wherever that is. I put Beethoven on in the background, prepared the rarebit, and read Granny Midgley's cookbook over breakfast. Those of us living in diaspora grow accustomed to physical separation from loved ones, for a diasporic existence can be isolating in that way; being cut off by decree intensifies that feeling even though nothing has changed—there is still social media and an increasing number of video chat platforms that sustain modern diasporic families. But somehow, imposed isolation feels different.

The English title, *Food for Today and Tomorrow*, is repeated in Sesotho: "lijo tsa kajeno le tsa hosanane". The front cover shows a young (presumably) Basotho child crouched in front of a fire on which sits a three-legged pot. In the background is the legae (home) and still further back, a view of the Maloti Mountains. A few pages of sponsor advertisements have been shoved in ahead of the title page, but once you reach it, you learn that the second edition was published by the Mazenod Institute in Maseru, Lesotho (then still Basutoland) in 1951. The first edition appeared during the Second World War.

The epigraph, "Le hosanane ke letsatsi" (Tomorrow is another day), echoes the title. Then comes the compiler's introduction. It is replete with words like "drought" and "pestilence", "unobtainable" and "unprocurable", and "thrift" and "economy". Those were the times. These are the times: words of war, depression, and pandemics infuse her introduction. I see that same language deployed with alarming casualness to describe the struggle to survive COVID-19. Not without cause, but I cannot help thinking that in the mouths of gormless, autocratic bullies such belligerent words seem hollow. I focus instead on the epigraph itself: tomorrow is another day.

We will survive, regardless. In places, the language of the compiler's note sits uncomfortably in today's world, but the advice seems searingly relevant to this moment:

"The natives of this vast land have their own ways of preserving and preparing food; they have learned through the ages, to rely only on what their country can produce and not on what may reach them from outside. This book has been specially designed to assist the European housewife who finds herself thrown upon her own resources in some lonely outpost, where it is still impossible to obtain foods other than the district can produce, owing to the difficulties of transport."

The importance of relying on locally sourced produce, on preservation, and the context of isolation and war is as relevant now as it was then. Lard drips from every page, I think as I tuck into tradition.

Granny Midgley's cookbook represents only one aspect of my culinary family history—the English side. I grew up in a bi-cultural, bilingual home, in a region of South Africa where the majority of the people spoke an Indigenous language that was not part of our home, but with whom I interacted daily even though racial segregation was official policy. To speak of "my heritage" is complicated. There are many facets to my existence, and cultural isolation here in Canada has polished them, too.

Ours is currently a multi-generational home: My daughter and her husband live upstairs in an apartment we built for them. Since we share the same space in isolation, she and I have taken the opportunity to bake together, as we did when she was younger. For recipes, we turn to another family cookbook. This is one my mother, her Ouma, made for each of her grandchildren. Ouma was a wonderful baker, and as a gift to her grandchildren, she wrote her favourite family recipes out by hand and gathered them in a binder. Whenever we open that collection of recipes, we connect with a different past: the bulk of the recipes are written in Afrikaans, my first language, and the language of my mother's people. By circumstance of marriage, my children did not grow up speaking Afrikaans in the home. What they know of my language they have gleaned from time spent among Afrikaans relatives. I make my daughter read the Afrikaans recipes so that she can learn to decipher her Ouma's words. We cook slowly, using the time to share stories and memories.

Ouma's recipes are very different from Granny Midgley's. Although Granny Midgley impresses on her readers to source locally, her recipes face outward, back across oceans to the Yorkshire moors of her people. Ouma's Afrikaans recipes face into the interior. This is boerekos—the native food of my mother's people. On that side of the family, we are of settler stock, but stock that has simmered into the African soil for centuries and that has been spiced with the aromas of the world. Ouma's recipes are a masala of curries from Malaysia and pastries from Holland, all infused over the centuries with the flavours of Africa.

I separate Granny Midgley's recipes from my mother's by the fact that they draw on an English heritage, but that is unfair. Her book is unabashedly local in the hints and substitutes she provides. The flavours of southern Africa bubble in the three-legged pot that graces the cover of Granny Midgley's book, and hint at another culinary tradition that brings together bits from all my pasts. A South African barbeque (braai) often consists of potjiekos—literally, "pot food." In basic terms, potjiekos is a stew cooked on an open fire in a three-legged pot. It is often accompanied by a stiff traditional maize porridge know as pap in Afrikaans, ting in Sesotho, or putu in isiXhosa. Pap is served with chakalaka, a spicy tomato-and-onion dipping sauce that draws on the flavours of East India. Both the imbiza (pot), and the pap are largely associated with Indigenous cooking, but over the years the three-legged pot has been ripped from its moorings beside the legae and placed on a more convenient stand in the suburbs, but its roots remain planted in the homestead. Here in Canada, a book of recipes for the potjie sits comfortably beside Ouma's book. As the current lockdown drags on, summer arrives, and with it comes the time to clean the pot.

As my daughter and I bake, I tell her stories of my youth, of sitting like that child on the cover of Granny Midgley's book, scooping putu from the imbiza with friends. I grew up during the apogee of apartheid, when the peoples of my country were separated by legislation. But over putu and a fire, children of all races bonded. That is where we roasted the creatures we'd trapped in the veld. It is these childhood friends who taught me to eat putu with skop: sheep's head baked in the ground under the fire. The name is a Xhosa neologistic contraction created from the Afrikaans—"skaap kop", or "sheep's head". The food that had travelled from the African pot into my family heritage has moved back to the ground from which it sprang through the sheep's head.

As I read Granny Midgley's book over my breakfast Welsh rarebit, I see a recipe for mulligatawny soup. Another memory wafts into the kitchen. Just across the road from Ma's florist shop—the old one in Taylor Street that burned down—was a small general dealer, Rama Mihta and Sons. Being of Indian descent in a small segregated Afrikaans community presented a different problem: the Mihtas had to send their son to boarding school since there was no place for him in the racially segregated schools of my hometown. But come holidays, Manoj and I would slip upstairs to the apartment above their shop and play, insulated from the apartheid world outside. There, we snacked on chivda and boondi while watching bootlegged tapes of Sampoorna Ramayana and listening to Lata Mangeshkar. In Manoj's home, spices became part of my culinary heritage, too. The smell of curries mingles and swirls onto the page in Ma's handwriting.

These are smells of home that have followed me to Canada. But today, we bake. Slowly, Afrikaans word by Afrikaans word, my daughter and I bring the food of our South African home to our Canadian home. Distances dissipate. With these smells, peace descends in troubled times. As the two of us cook and bake in Afrikaans, she tells me she is pregnant, and I find additional comfort in the knowledge that these recipes, these snippets of Afrikaans, Sesotho, and isiXhosa—the languages of my parents' childhood, and of my own childhood—will be passed on to my children's children.

Culinary Geographies

Yasser Abdellatif (*Egypt*)
Egyptian Cuisine: Historical and Geographical Features

Maitham Salman (*Iraq*)
Masgouf: The Crown of Iraqi Cuisine

Egyptian Cuisine: Historical and Geographical Features

Yasser Abdellatif

    To talk about food in such a multicultural context as the present anthology, is to talk about Geography: about location and climate, winds and rain, rivers and seas, crops and fruits, cattle and livestock. For the diet of a region is the hardware to its cuisine (the software).

    Egypt belongs to the Mediterranean Basin nations, it is located in the northeastern corner of Africa, but if you look at the map, you will notice that the Northern coast of Egypt on the Mediterranean is positioned two degrees of latitude more to the south, compared to all its Arab neighbours around the Southern and Eastern banks of that rectangular basin, except for Libya. As a consequence of this geographical fact it has lost the climate moderation typical of that basin, in favour of the African Saharan heat. The loss, however, is not absolute, at least it touches the reigning crop of this ecological system: olives. As a consequence, Egypt lost the abundance of its precious golden oil. This Good Cholesterol type of fat is the keystone of the regional cuisines, from Morocco to Syria, and from Turkey to Portugal around that sea lying in the centre of the old world. Thus, Egypt lost its membership in the world's healthiest alimentary hardware, the famous Mediterranean diet.

Egypt used to be an important producer of olives and wine around the time of the Byzantine Empire. Historians and meteorologists have told us about significant climate change between the third and sixth centuries AD that affected the whole northern hemisphere, including the Mediterranean Basin. Due to this change, the production of those two crops deteriorated quantitatively and qualitatively. We still have olive and wine production, but not as good as the Algerian or the Syrian regions, not to mention the Italian or Spanish.

Today, the life span of Egyptian citizens averages seventy-one-and-a-half years, compared to eighty-two for the Lebanese, and seventy-six for Algerians. Considering other factors such as prosperity levels, rates of pollution, and the quality of health services, the diet factor contributes largely to these numbers, since heart disease is the most frequent cause of death in Egypt.

Egyptian cuisine relies on cattle's fat and butter, sesame, and cottonseed oil. The primary source of protein in the Egyptian kitchen has always been bovine meat (mouton to a less degree), poultry, dairy, and legumes. Swine was never desirable, even before the introduction of Islam. It is believed Judaism introduced to Islam the prohibition of eating pork. Hebrews, in turn, inherited it from Ancient Egyptians, much like the religious rite of male circumcision, as Sigmund Freud tried to prove in his book *Moses and Monotheism*. The priests of Egypt equated pigs to the evil god Seth, or Lion Scare, the bad uncle of the Egyptian Holy Family. Also for theological reasons, it was not favourable to eat female bovine—the cow represented the Goddess Isis, the mother of the same family.

Water buffaloes were introduced into Egypt around the middle of the seventh century, in synchronicity with the Arabic Invasion, and the slow religious transformation to Islam. Buffaloes have lived in the Nile Delta and Valley since then, along with their bovine cousins, adding a rich source of protein from dairy and meat to Egyptian cuisine. People prefer buffalo milk over that of cow's, because of its richness and the thick cream and butter it produces, while the buffalo's veal is considered the most precious meat in the market.

Beef or lamb stews, with vegetables or legumes, have been the main staple of Egyptian lunches throughout history, from 2500 BC until now. White rice (introduced to the Nile Valley in the same 7th century), or Vermicelli rice, usually accompanies those stews nowadays, sparing bread for breakfast and dinner, meals of less social importance in urban middle-class life.

Long-shoot green onions have been a constant element in the food culture of the Nile valley since ancient times. Unlike Chinese and Indians, Egyptians commonly don't cook it. They're consumed fresh as appetizers, chopped in green salads, or whole, biting the white bulb down to the green ferny leaves. Cooked green onions rarely appear, and when they do, they are shredded with dill, leeks, and parsley, then added to ground fava beans, shaped into small balls, then deep-fried as croquettes in oil—Felafel, or Ta'meyya as the dish is known in Cairo. Felafel in the Levant does not call for green onions; instead it is made from grounded chickpeas, rather than fava beans. Spring onions have religious symbolic value inherited from Pharaonic mythology. They are an essential element in the celebration of the Shemu feast, which comes the Monday after the Coptic Easter. On this spring festival, fermented, salted mullet fish is served with spring onion. Fish in such a state alludes to death and mummification, while green onions symbolize revitalization and growth. In this Egyptian Holy Week, pharaonic beliefs merge with eastern Christianity. The Father, the Son, and the Holy Ghost are reflected in the mirrors of the Ancient Egyptian trinity of Isis, Osiris, and their son Horus.

For breakfast, Foul Medammes, fava beans slow-cooked and usually tossed with sesame oil, a hint of lime juice, and cumin is the iconic national dish that unifies all the social classes. Better-off households will substitute the sesame oil with butter or olive oil. Foul is typically served with whole-grain wheat bread called Baladi. Along with its deep-fried sister Felafel and salad or pickles. Foul is also the ubiquitous staple of the less-privileged classes which sometimes are forced to consume it three times a day as a substitute for other meals, because of its affordability.

According to the region, or cultural character, breakfast also may consist of different types of bread, such as buttered dough Meshaltet, or crispy flat Bettao, widely consumed in rural areas. Fine baguette-like loaves and pita bread are common in major cities and among middle-class families. All those types of bread are suitable to pair with local cottage cheese, fresh or aged and mixed with tahini; white saltier cheese flavoured with hot green pepper, or the queen of Egyptian dairy products: Roumi cheese, drifted from Italian Parmesan, with a stronger taste. Halva, honey, or different types of jams can also be present here with fresh cream, and of course, eggs in all their variations, much like any other place in the world.

Cornered northeast of Africa and southeast of the Mediterranean, Egypt is positioned at the crossroad of several cultures and diets. Besides its ambiguous culinary relationship with the Mediterranean, Egypt's diet is influenced by Bedouin food culture from the east across the Red Sea, East African cuisine, and Ethiopian lineaments spread all the way north through Sudan until Nubia and Upper Egypt. The Arabic Bedouin cuisine staple consists of Fatta or Thareed, large mounds of rice cooked with abundant portions of lamb, beef, or chicken, sometimes mixed with roasted flakes of bread. Egyptians consume these dishes particularly at family banquets during the Islamic feast of Grand Bayram, a testament to the country's attachment to the culture of the Arabic peninsula. In southern Egypt, East African influences appear in an assortment of thin fermented bread, a variation on the famous Ethiopian Injera, cured meat cooked in spicy tomato sauce, with dried okra, and other types of vegetables.

Currents of cultures and layers of mythological and religious heritage have shaped Egyptian cuisine, though it doesn't have a visible presence in the food industry abroad. Unlike their neighbours, the Lebanese and Levanters (the grandsons of Phoenicians) who form the core of the Arabic communities in North America; and the North Africans from Maghreb (the grandsons of Carthaginians) amongst the most significant populations of immigrants in Europe, Egyptians were not great mariners and traders. The main characteristic of the Egyptian personality is the settled villager who prefers to farm a piece of land around the Nile, rather than travel and take the risk of an adventure.

In Canada, the majority of the Egyptian community consists of urban professionals (physicians, engineers, or academics). Like their farmer ancestors, they favour a stable income style of life, with no inclination towards business, trade, or investments. I believe this lifestyle choice is the reason behind the scarcity of Egyptian restaurants in North America. Egypt is a country that has always been better at receiving people, incorporating their lifestyles into its ancient traditions, rather than sending immigrants to other parts of the world.

Masgouf: The Crown of Iraqi Cuisine

Maitham Salman

Origins:

Masgouf is the typical Iraqi dish reminiscent of my home country; more so than any other Iraqi dishes. I had enjoyed Masgouf before leaving Iraq for good at the age of twenty-seven. Masgouf, or grilling fish in Masgouf style, is never found in any food court. This national dish has been part of the Mesopotamian kitchen for thousands of years rooted in the Sumerian civilization from Southern Iraq. The word Masgouf means in the Aramaic language "Impaled"—in this case, it means impaling the fish with two wedges in order to have it stand before an open fire. Masgouf has its own rituals; it is not just putting a fish before the fire to be grilled! It requires a specific process and several conditions including but not limited to the size of the fish and the way to consume it.

Recipe:

The best fish with which to make Masgouf in Iraq are Binni (common barbel) or Shabbout (common carp). These two fatty and high-quality types of freshwater fish exist in the waters of the Tigris and Euphrates rivers. They also live in many of their tributaries. The ideal size for Masgouf must be no less than one kilogram. The fish must be sliced open along the backbone, so it lies completely flat, and to make sure the thick area around the backbone is cooked evenly. Opening the fish this way makes it look like a large disk, leaving the belly intact. Then it is partially scaled, gutted, and gilled. The next step calls for making two small cuts in the back of the fish—around two centimeters wide—just enough to hang it over the two standing wedges.

Some people prefer only rock salt for seasoning, while others like to add lemon or black pepper. Some chefs like to use firewood from citrus trees to add a tart, smoky aroma to the taste. Others choose to let the fish rest for five minutes, then hang it over the two wedges horizontally at about fifty centimetres before an open fire. The fish looks as if it stands on its side so it can receive heat evenly. It takes around forty-five minutes until most of the fish's fat is burned off and the top looks crispy. The tempting amber hue moves the fish to its final stage, putting it on the back directly over some burning coal for only five minutes to crisp the skin as well. Now the mouth-watering fish is fully cooked; aromatic, caramelized on top, and tender from the inside.

How to Eat Masgouf:

Iraqis, who like to eat fish on Wednesdays and Fridays as tradition, present Masgouf with Iraqi Tanoor bread (like naan bread), green onion, tomato, and pickles. Typically, Iraqis lay the whole fish in a tray garnished with lime and slices of onion and tomato. A luscious meal. Connoisseurs of Masgouf recommend the dish to be eaten with bare hands, not fork and knife, to appreciate its flavour and texture better. If you don't dig in with your fingers to scoop the juicy flakes, you don't savour the supreme taste of Masgouf to its full effect.

Passion:

Masgouf is one of the foods that unites all Iraqis, all of whom crave it regardless of where they live, their ethnicity, or religion. Whether they are poor or wealthy, ordinary citizens or the president. Iraqi former president, Saddam Hussein, was known for his high affection for Masgouf. This very dish led to his capture by American Occupation Forces six months after they invaded Iraq in April of 2003. According to Eric Maddox (the Army interrogation specialist who led the hunt for Hussein), Saddam Hussein was tracked down through the trail of Masgouf. Maddox learned from Hussein's special chef that Masgouf was his boss' favourite dish. And because the ousted dictator and his inner circle all were being followed closely, they couldn't purchase fish from the markets directly. One of Hussein's close associates told Maddox that Hussein had ordered some of his guards to dig a fishpond and fill it with carp fish and one of the fishermen at this pond had disclosed the place where Hussein's bodyguard was hiding. That fisherman was the one leading the special search team to the man who ruled Iraq for twenty-four years.

Nostalgia:

As for me, an Iraqi who has lived abroad since 1997, Masgouf reminds me of my best days while attending classes at the University of Baghdad. I used to go to Abu Nuwas Street, which runs along the east bank of the Tigris across the so-called Green Zone. Named after the great Arab poet Abu Nuwas al-Hakami (AD 756–814), renowned for his fondness of wine and fun, it is the most famous street in Iraq. The street, known for the best Masgouf restaurants in the country, has more than twenty restaurants and many bars. Any of these Masgouf restaurants has a concrete tub covered with ceramic tiles and filled with fish, along with a clay oven (Tanoor) for Iraqi flat bread. On a podium-like sandbox off the ground (a metre high) built from concrete and topped with soil, there is a large fire in the middle, encircled by wooden or metal foot-long poles, pinned to the soil about a foot apart from each other. When a customer chooses a fish, the chef prepares it especially for them by placing it over any two poles for less than an hour, obtaining the most flavourful smoked fish.

I'll never forget wandering with friends along this street in the wee hours, adoring the dreamlike aroma of blazing firewood, yearning for the enticing scent of Masgouf suspended on sticks forming a circle of fish as if around a campfire. This very scene washes over me, a wave of nostalgia. In Edmonton, I try to replicate the process of grilling and smoking to make Masgouf as close to the authentic dish as possible. Mrigal and Rohu, frozen fish imported from Myanmar, available in some stores in Edmonton south are the stand-in for the real thing. In the summertime, I use my fire pit in the backyard to make Masgouf. During the wintertime, I use my charcoal grill in the garage—putting the fish in a grill basket. In my second hometown, I've found a way to overcome this longing.

Culinary Politics

Mila Bongco-Philipzig (*Philippines*)
Disposable Double Double Lives

Asma Sayed (*India*)
Of Curries and Custard Apples: Identity, Memory, Resistance

Tazeen Hasan (*Pakistan*)
Biryani, Beef Lynchings, and the Kristallnacht of India

Ana Ruiz Aguirre (*Cuba*)
Resolviendo

Disposable Double Double Lives
Mila Bongco-Philipzig

In 2014, a week after my son turned fourteen, he started working at a fast food counter in Edmonton City Centre Mall. At that time, the food court was located in the basement, and all the fast food stalls formed a circle around the middle seating area. There were Filipino temporary foreign workers (TFWs) working in almost all of the stalls. I knew only one of them, but the Filipino workers in the food court all knew each other. Quickly, they learned about my young son working at McDonalds.

About three weeks after my son started, I waited to pick him up until past the mall's closing time. All the stalls emptied, and the grilled gates were drawn to block off the food court area. I had no way to know where my son was. I peered through the grills worriedly until a Filipino custodian came out with a mop, saw me, then deliberately walked over. He said my son was still inside, washing up the floors and kitchen sinks at McD. I had never met this man before, yet he knew me and my son, and took the time to assuage me.

As I frequented this food court to pick up my son, I got to know more of the Filipino foreign workers there. Truly heartwarming to me, they repeatedly said that they were keeping an eye out for my son and that he could have freebies from them. During his breaks, he could walk through the food court and would get offered a cookie here, some tacos there, a slice of pizza, some teriyaki beef with rice—what a treat! I felt we had stumbled upon a community invisible to most Canadians, but which brought back memories of growing up in a little village in the Philippines. The summer I was five, my siblings and I stayed with our grandma. In the wet market, we knew exactly which stalls to go to for free stuff: a free coconut bun or a square of kalamay (sticky rice), a glass of sago and gulaman, or a stick of banana que (fried, sugared plaintain). Once, we even got free rubber slippers! Only later did I find out, these people knew our mother left us earlier that year and were actually giving us little tokens of affection. I felt the Filipinos working at the food court were doing the same for my son whom they had never met before. What were the chances that the saying, "It takes a village to raise a child" would play out in a Canadian food court for us?

I was also elated to find out that many of the TFWs cooked extremely well and accepted orders. Suddenly, I had access to traditional Philippine food that was not readily available in Edmonton at that time: pancit palabok, molo, laing, bicol express, kare-kare, dinuguan, menudo, mechado, chicken pastel, empanada, cassava cake, sapin-sapin, turon, and so on. I started eating lunch more and more often in that food court, enjoying traditional Philippine food, as well as sharing memories and stories with my heritage community. And without knowing how to cook myself, I became a star at potluck parties.

After I helped one of the TFWs gather documents and write a letter to obtain a visitor visa to Canada for her mother, some other workers came to me for assistance in documentation, letter-writing, and understanding policies on employment, benefits, and becoming a permanent resident in Canada. I got to know them better as they confided in me more and more. I was dismayed and alarmed to find out about their plight as TFWs. Many of them had gone into debt in order to pay some placement agency to come over. The TFWs had left parents, siblings, spouses, and children, putting their lives on hold for the chance to work for low or minimum wages in Canada. Each and every one came hoping to become a permanent resident at the end of their contract, and to bring the rest of their family over to Canada. Unfortunately, it was not made clear to them that this would be extremely difficult, and in many cases impossible.

When Canada started the Temporary Foreign Workers Programme (TFWP) in 1973, its main objective was to fill short-term labour shortages for live-in caregivers, seasonal agricultural workers, and skilled workers in the fields of IT, nursing, research, and so on. I myself came on a student visa in 1984 and after completing a master's degree, was eligible to apply for permanent residency. Starting in 2002, however, changes in the TFWP added recruitment in the Low-Skills category. The change to include low- and minimum-wage occupations was a major turning point from Canada's traditional immigration policy that allowed temporary foreign workers to eventually apply for permanent residency.

Under the new policy, the direct path to Canadian citizenship was gone. TFWs now entered the country with temporary contracts tied to one particular employer. In order to keep a work permit, renew a contract, or be eligible to apply for permanent status, they needed the support of their employer—a vulnerable and exploitable position to be in. As a result, TFWs were often scared to speak out about exploitative work, unacceptable living conditions, and the precariousness of their status in Canada. TFWs often found themselves in cramped living conditions, for example, five to seven people sharing a two-bedroom basement, paying rents far higher than market value to their employers as the money was automatically deducted from their pay. Some were not paid for overtime worked, were compelled to work over holidays, and often refused adequate time off. Some TFWs were required to do additional manual work for their employers outside the scope of what they were hired for. Some found themselves in small towns where they had to endure racial slurs and disdain. Yet despite these hardships and injustices, there seemed to be an unending supply of Filipino TFWs in the food courts and fast food diners in Edmonton, and to some degree, all over Alberta. Indeed, from 2000 to 2011, there was a noticeable increase in the numbers of TFWs in Alberta: it jumped from around 9,500 in 2000 to over 65,000 in 2011. At the peak of TFW hiring between 2007 and 2011, the Philippines was the largest source of international migrant labour for western Canada, providing people to work mostly as meat packers, food counter attendants, and hotel room service staff.

In addition to the 2002 changes in the TFWP, the rapid rise of Filipino TFWs in Alberta can be attributed to the following factors:
  a) the oil boom in Alberta circa 2005–2014
  b) the expansion and fast-tracking of temporary workers in the fast food, hotel, and meat packing industries in 2006 onwards
  c) Tim Hortons' pivotal role in shaping the Stream for Low-Skilled Occupations (S-LSO), as well as its target recruitment from the Philippines
  d) the systemic complicity of the Philippine administration for international labour brokering.

The Philippine government played an active part in providing migrant workers internationally, and to Canada specifically. Since the 1990s, the Philippines had increasingly benefitted from the remittances sent by overseas workers. The government started to intentionally research global labour markets to identify anticipated shortages. TESDA (Technical Education and Skills Development Authority) was established to provide training programmes to align with the global demands, purposefully creating culture-and industry-specific Filipino workers appropriate for export to host destinations. In her book, *Marketing Dreams, Manufacturing Heroes: The Transnational Labor Brokering of Filipino Workers*, Anna Guevarra shows how the Philippine state and employment agencies actively marketed and manufactured a social imaginary of the Philippines as the "Home of the Great Worker." It was subtly instilled among Filipinos that they should be disciplined and loyal migrant workers because they had the responsibility to their country and families to support and sustain this manufactured image of the "Great Filipino Worker." Instead of systematically addressing the lack of opportunities and unacceptably high unemployment in the country, the Philippine state deliberately instilled desires in Filipinos to work overseas, hailing them as modern-day heroes for consistently sending back remittances which have propped up the economy.

But more than just being able to work and send money back

home, many migrant workers dream of relocating permanently to a country more developed and affluent than the Philippines for a better life for themselves and their families. With this mindset, Canada had always been at the top of work destinations for Filipinos, second only to the US and high above countries in Asia and the Middle East. The migration history between Canada and the Philippines in the 1960s and 1970s—when Filipinos came over as nurses, garment workers, live-in caregivers, and eventually became permanent residents—created the prevalent thinking among TFWs that migration to Canada was almost guaranteed at the end of a work contract. The desire to migrate permanently to Canada resulted in the pervasiveness of Filipinos coming over to work as TFWs in Alberta starting in the early 2000s until the present.

The strong preference for Canada among the Filipino TFWs played into the hands of Tim Hortons' need for "suitable" fast food workers. Around 2006, Tim Hortons convinced the Canadian government that there was a labour shortage in the tourism/hospitality industry in western Canada. Tim Hortons lobbied aggressively and succeeded in having low-wage occupations be included in the TFWP. This gave rise to the Low-Skilled Pilot Project (LSPP) which later became the Stream for Low-Skill Occupations (S-LSO). Tim Hortons' involvement was so crucial and conspicuous that Aida Polanco Sorto, an Assistant Professor in Labour Studies, writes in her doctoral thesis that, "over the years, government bureaucrats jokingly referred to the LSPP or S-LSO as the 'Tim Hortons Programme'" (*Behind the Counter: Migration, Labour Policy and Temporary Work in a Global Fast Food Chain* p. 33). Many studies and articles have since indicated that there was no actual labour shortage but that fast food and hotel staff positions attracted only "undesirable workers"—students, older people, or newcomers—who were not motivated nor fast enough, or who would resign when the work became difficult. The newcomers specifically were not yet attuned to the Canadian culture or not linguistically capable of fast-paced or customer-facing work.

Tim Hortons recognized quickly that finding willing and motivated workers from the Philippines was as easy as it was profitable. Not only were Filipinos culturally and linguistically equipped for Canada, but there were lots of highly qualified, able-bodied, docile, and loyal workers to choose from since many Filipinos were eager to work in Canada. The national stereotype of the "Great Worker" fed the Tim Hortons counters so effectively that the company increasingly took over the direct recruitment of workers from the Philippines, bypassing recruitment agencies and taking over their franchises' applications.

Tim Hortons could have recruited from any part of the world but recruited more than 50 percent of their workforce from the Philippines. By 2010, 77.76 percent of its workers recruited from abroad came from the Philippines. Tim Hortons could be choosy and still import the best, most desirable workers for difficult, minimum wage jobs.

But why were Filipinos so eager to work for low pay in frigid Alberta? Work was scarce in the Philippines, and the standard of living was far lower than in Canada. Even at minimum wage in Alberta, TFWs could earn more here to support their families back home (for comparison, the median wage for a high school teacher in Metro Manila in 2015 was $400.00/month). And ultimately, Filipino TFWs were prepared to disrupt their lives and families for the elusive promise of being able to settle permanently in Canada, a belief based on previous immigration history between the two countries.

The end of the oil boom in Alberta in 2014 and the weakening of the economy exposed how disposable TFWs truly were. In 2015, changes to the TFW program introduced more bureaucracy and longer processes, shorter work permits, no contract extensions, as well as provisions that clearly prevented TFWs from being able to settle here. No matter how long a TFW had previously worked in Canada, the message was clear: they now had to leave. TFWs' lives and status became even more precarious as some were caught in between the policy changes, employers failed to comply with new documentation requirements or processes, jobs became more scarce, permits expired, extensions were not allowed, the nomination for skilled worker status became more stringent, and so on. The changes caught many TFWs unprepared. Some had given birth to a child while in Canada but were nevertheless not allowed to stay. Some chose to stay anyway to join the underground economy, cognizant of the lack of jobs in the Philippines or needing to repay the money borrowed to come over. Undocumented, they became further marginalized and open to exploitation.

Now there is a COVID-19 pandemic. Social distancing is imposed. By April 2020, almost everything declared a non-essential business is closed, but businesses that supply the food chain must remain open. There is an outbreak at the Cargill Meat Plant in Alberta. Over 900 workers have been infected, and two people have died. Seventy percent of workers in the meat plant are Filipinos. There is backlash against the community from Canadians who believe the TFWs were responsible. The Filipinos feel unfairly blamed for the outbreak, as comments are made about carpooling and inter-generational or multi-family households. Workers claim that proper PPE was not provided, physical distancing was not enforced, and they were required to show up for work even if they were sick. After the plant is closed for a week, there is pressure to go back to work even though there are no reassurances that proper measures and changes will be applied to prevent further contagion. The workers—many TFWs, some undocumented—are afraid to lose their jobs but are also anxious about getting sick and dying.

The pandemic throws into focus who the essential workers are outside of healthcare services and utilities: meat packers, grocery staff, custodial workers, cleaners, fast food attendants, and others in similar occupations that pay mostly minimum or low wages, many of them filled by TFWs. Data from the UK and USA indicate that there is a higher rate of contagion and death among ethnic minorities, but Canada does not yet collect race-based data related to COVID-19. The precariousness of migrant lives intensifies where illness and death are the potential results of working and living conditions over which they have no control.

I have lost touch with many of the TFWs I met downtown when the City Centre mall food court underwent renovations in the summer of 2015. Even before that, there was already a lot of turnover as contracts expired and other TFWs took their places. The new food court in downtown Edmonton opened in November 2016 at the top floor of the mall with soaring skylights, bright, white tiles, and modern tables and seats. It was three times bigger than the old one. There were still Filipino TFWs but noticeably much fewer. Meanwhile, I had established close ties with Migrante Alberta which is part of an alliance of Filipino groups across Canada helping to address the worsening conditions for foreign and migrant workers.

In the middle of a pandemic, the City Centre Mall food court is eerily empty and quiet as only some stalls are open for take-out. None of the background chatter in Tagalog nor the ethnic dishes and bursts of laughter shared in the old space. My son is now enrolled at the University of Alberta and I have since moved to another job and gotten a promotion. But my TFW friends were not as lucky. There is neither permanence nor upward mobility afforded to TFWs. Federal and provincial policies regarding migrant workers consistently favour the employers. Foreign workers are mostly deemed replaceable, as disposable as the cups for our double doubles.

Of Curries and Custard Apples: Identity, Memory, Resistance

Asma Sayed

It is May 1998. I am a new immigrant to Canada having arrived in Edmonton after landing in Vancouver. I, with my husband, am staying at a friend's house while we find a good rental place for us. We go out each day to see a condo or two; we were looking for a clean, lighted place as we were expecting our first child in four months. One fine evening, a building manager opens an apartment for us to consider. As we enter the apartment, he says: "This is a good place, but you are not allowed to make curry in here. Other people in the building will not like the strong smell of your food." We did not complete our tour of the apartment. Of course, we were going to make curry, and whatever else we wanted to, in our home. I learnt much later that such xenophobic dictates of what we should eat in our own home were not too uncommon in those days. What good would it be to be in a house where we cannot cook what is close to our culture, identity, and self? I had just left behind my country, my home, my family, my friends. Now, I was being asked to give up my food. That wasn't happening. After all, food is part of our identity, who we are, where we come from, and who we become. It ties our past, present, and future. We found another rental place where questions about our culinary identities were not asked, and we cooked curry, and whatever our hearts desired, in that condo which we rented for nearly a year and a half. When food is politicised, what we consume is our resistance.

What I found amusing in that encounter with the apartment manager was that he asked only about curry which he identified as "your food." Without knowing anything about me other than the fact that I had just arrived from India, he assumed that all the people from India eat curry, that curry is a staple Indian diet. Curry became symbolic of my ethnic identity. This stereotype about Indian gastronomy is rampant and sometimes used to the advantage to attract customers to Indian restaurants; just look at some of the restaurant names in Edmonton and across Canada: The Curry House; The Curry Kitchen; The Curry Corner; Kurry Kebab; Curry Twist, and on and on. Yet, the reality is that Indian cuisine is extremely diverse just as the country is. People in the north of India eat very different food from those in the south. Wheat is part of the staple diet in the north, but those in the south generally prefer a rice-based diet. Eastern Indians use more seafood, and western India has more vegetarian options. I am simplifying a bit here, but you get the point. Food culture in India, and thus in its diaspora, is much more complex. Curry's position as central to an Indian diet is over-rated if not misleading. Naben Ruthnum, a Canadian author and cultural critic, in his book, *Curry: Eating, Reading, and Race* (2017), offers a very interesting argument about the way curry seems to unite and serve as a symbol for South Asian culture, while also falsely perpetuating the myth of a singular culture that obliterates the vast and diverse cultural-scape and associated flavours, fragrances, and colours which are part and parcel of the ethos. Ruthnum writes that there is no single 'authentic' curry, and yet, it has come to assume an identity for South Asians in diaspora. At the same time, Ruthnum argues that the metaphor is overused and has its limitations: "Thinking about and writing about a food as culturally complex as curry as though it were a marker of an authentic past that is now lost, or a signifier of a broken bond between generations due to geographical dislocation, does a major disservice to how delicious curry is, and to how particular a South Asian diasporic experience can be."[1] There is so much more to India and its gastronomic traditions which vary from region to region.

I was born and raised in the Gujarat province in India. Gujarati cuisine has a very distinct flavour and aroma. It is known for its simple vegetarian meals comprising of roti (flatbread); curry; daal-chaaval (lentil soup, usually made of toor daal and rice); snacks such as khaman dhokla and mathia; special meals such as undhiyu which is a spicy medley of vegetables cooked in a clay pot; sweets such as penda and shrikhand. While roti made of wheat is common for an afternoon meal, flatbreads made out of millet flour, known as bajra ni rotli, substitute for wheat roti in many households. Gujarati food is simultaneously sweet and salty, spicy and flavourful. Spicy pickles and buttermilk are usually part of an afternoon meal especially in summer. Some Gujaratis, particularly non-Hindus, do consume non-vegetarian diet, but Gujarati cuisine's uniqueness is in its vegetarian fare; this too varies across regions within Gujarat. I wasn't much of a cook when I lived in India, and neither am I much of a foodie. When I need comfort, a simple Gujarati daal-chaaval is enough. This simple, day-to-day meal is not that easy to find in restaurants in Canada which usually serve what people don't necessarily eat on a daily basis at home. I could not find Gujarati food at restaurants in Edmonton in 1998. Even now, in 2020, there is no dedicated Gujarati restaurant in the city although it is known for its elaborate range of eateries and festivals. I hear that many Gujarati families in Edmonton are now running tiffin services from home, but it is near impossible to find Gujarati delicacies in Edmonton's South Asian restaurants, which mostly serve Punjabi fare, despite a sizeable Gujarati population. Vancouver and Toronto have many restaurants specifically dedicated to Gujarati cuisine. The closest other option that Gujaratis choose is South Indian food which also has many vegetarian varieties. South India's rice-, lentil-, and coconut-based diet has a great appeal to vegetarians. Idli, dosa, vada, and sambhar, along with coconut chutney are usually part of a South Indian meal irrespective of the time of the day. As much as South Indian dishes were not easily available in the 90s, there are a few South Indian food joints in Edmonton now, my favourite being Savoy's South Indian Kitchen on 34th Avenue in the area that has come to be known as Little India.

Come summer, Gujarati meals would be incomplete without pulp from either Kesar or Alphonso mangoes. In fact, mangoes are all the rage in India from March to June. Now also used by internationally renowned chefs such as Yotam Ottolenghi, Alphonso is considered the king of mangoes, or the king of fruit, in India. If you haven't tasted an Alphonso, you haven't lived. Some may argue that Kesar mango is better, but my personal favourite is Alphonso. Both varieties are grown in western India. Named after Afonso de Albuquerque, a Portuguese colonizer in India, Alphonso is a mixed breed. Famously known as the fruit sent to London for the Queen's coronation in 1953, Alphonso is used in many desserts and drinks. It is unparalleled given its bright yellow colour, its strong fragrance, juiciness, and the sweetness which is from heaven. For years, every summer, I pined for Alphonso in Edmonton. Now, they are not very difficult to get. Every week in summer, a consignment comes in from India full of packages of mangoes which are then available at stores in Little India. They go off the shelf in hours, if not minutes. That is why I book my boxes in advance. The price is steep, but worth it. The magic of mango, a few weeks each summer, makes India and its memories become livelier in my house.

Speaking of fruits, my other favourite, which is nearly impossible to find in Edmonton, is custard apple generally known as sitafal in India. I am still very surprised to know that the majority of people here in Edmonton, and more broadly in Canada, have never even heard about this fruit. I was overjoyed last year when I found it while visiting the Granville Island Market in British Columbia. I bought a few although they were almost ten dollars apiece. I have also introduced this fruit to a few of my friends. Custard apple reminds me of my aunt-in-law whom we lovingly called Dadima. There is a huge custard apple tree, a few decades old, in the backyard of my in-laws' massive haweli in Junagadh at the footsteps of the Gir forest in the Gujarat province. Every summer, we would harvest a huge load of custard apples, that is, whatever was left after hordes of monkeys who live in the nearby Gir forest had had their fill. When I briefly lived in Junagadh, Dadima, knowing that I loved custard apples, would go get a few from the tree while they were still unripe and hide them for me in large wheat containers where they ripened nicely but were also hidden from others in the house. Now that I live between Edmonton and Vancouver, I regularly go in search of custard apples at the Granville Island Market. Memories of Dadima, who has now left this earthly abode, Junagadh, the Gir, Gujarat, home, love, and so much more, the said and the unsaid, come alive with these apples that require much patience to eat given their very seedy structure. Recollections of culinary spaces, fragrances, and gastronomic practices can be nostalgic.

Food is central to cultural life, especially for diaspora subjects like me who have moved from one place to another. It not only sustains our ties to the home left behind, but also helps to create a new home space in our adopted land. It triggers memories of places and people, friends and families. For people in diaspora, food can also be a reminder of their 'otherness' especially if it is not considered part of the 'mainstream' culinary trends. In fact, in multi-ethnic countries such as Canada, diasporic culinary cultures are often invoked as symbolic of diversity and inclusion thus leading to 'celebratory multiculturalism' which naively exoticizes certain outward components of culture such as food, clothing, dance, and music, while ignoring entrenched social inequities.[2] Take, for example, Edmonton's Heritage Festival. There are many good things about this festival, but it also gives people a false sense of being inclusive. The various South Asian tents—including India, Pakistan, Bangladesh, and Sri Lanka—serve stereotypical chick peas, mango lassi, and samosas, to name a few things. Non-South Asian people eat these few tidbits and go home with the satisfaction of having had a taste of South Asian culture. That is the irony! Adoring a few dance moves and sampling a few stereotypical 'national' dishes leads to superficial multiculturalism.

Fast forward to 2019. I have organized a party for a few of my friends. After all, they keep asking: "Asma, when can we come to have some of your biryani?" None of these friends are South Asian. They love my Indian cooking. At many parties that I now attend, samosa has become a favourite finger food. South Asian diet was considered messy and smelly for a long time. But the contributions of many restaurateurs, such as Vikram Vij with his multiple eateries and success as one of Canada's top chefs, have changed the

Canadian, and global, culinary landscape and led to the popularity of South Asian food. South Asian restaurants in Edmonton have mushroomed in the last decade and they are thriving: most of them visited regularly by non-South Asian folks. I sometimes think about that building manager who showed me the apartment. I wonder if he still finds Indian food smelly, stinky, or if he has warmed up to global food cultures, if he has broadened his way of looking at people and the world at large. I hope he is not missing out on the global culinary fare that Edmonton restaurants now offer, albeit with their limitations.

NOTES

1. Ruthnum, Naben. *Curry: Eating, Reading, and Race* (Toronto: Coach House, 2017), 24.

2. I have explored at length some of the ideas presented in this piece in my article "Writing Beyond Curry-Books: Construction of Racialized and Gendered Diasporic Identities in Anita Rau Badami's *Can You Hear the Nightbird Call?*" published in: Boyd, Shelley and Dorothy Barenscott, eds. *Canadian Culinary Imaginations* (Montreal: McGill-Queen's University Press, 2020), 277-94.

Tazeen Hasan
Biryani, Beef Lynchings, and the Kristallnacht of India

Widening her curious dark brown eyes, my seven-year-old daughter once asked, "Mom how do you make Biryani so quickly when other women take so long?" Standing in front of the stove, frying up the onion, in my kitchen in the Red Sea coastal city of Duba, Northern Saudi Arabia, I couldn't respond to her query at first. I later told her that when I was pregnant with her, I would make Biryani almost every day for weeks as it was the food I craved the most and no other food was able to treat my morning sickness. As a Pakistani born daughter of Muslim immigrants from India, the love of this world class South Asian—and now continental—delicacy is etched in my nerves.

A blend of saffron and white-coloured large grain basmati rice steamed in layers and layers of tenderized meat, suffused with thick heavy dark brown gravy made up of caramelized onions, an intricate mix of exotic spices, mint, green chilies, and coriander, effuses an irresistible aroma. People say making Biryani is an art not everyone can master, no matter how expensive the spices and food items used for its preparation.

The story goes that Biryani originated in Persia or Central

Asia. The rice and meat dish that came from the greater Persian world, however, was Pulao not Biryani. The rice in Pulao is boiled in meat stock while in Biryani it is simmered with thick spicy gravy. Central Asian Pulao is different from the South Asian version. Last year, I was in Istanbul during the Muslim holy month of Ramadan living with some Central Asian Uyghur families from Xinjiang, China's northwestern province. I attended many iftar feasts with them. What I missed in their Pulao were the spices and aroma that come with the Pulao made in the subcontinent. Whether Biryani arrived from Persia or not, its name surely does. "Biryan" is a Persian word meaning fried or roasted. Nonetheless, it is the first food that comes to mind when outsiders think of South Asian food. One study says Biryani is the most ordered food on Swiggy, the largest food delivery app in India. In 2014, the dish dominated the news, when popular Indian cricketer Mahendra Singh Dhoni had to switch hotels in Hyderabad, India, because his former hotel did not allow him to bring Biryani from outside. No doubt, Biryani is India's most popular dish on the internet world-wide. However, despite its popularity, this crown of Indian culinary tradition has become a constant part of the Indian political discourse in the current polarizing atmosphere. Politicians are using Biryani to discredit rivals. In 2019, opposition leader Priyanka Gandhi accused Prime Minister Modi for going to Pakistan to eat Biryani.

According to a *Times of India* article published in 2015, Ujjwal Nikam, the prosecutor in the Mumbai terror-attack case (a.k.a. India's 9/11), revealed and admitted that he had concocted the story that the alleged Pakistani terrorist, Ajmal Kasab, demanded Biryani in the prison cell, in order to break the emotional atmosphere in favour of Kasab during the trial. A dish being used to villainize an alleged terrorist? This is enough evidence that despite the irresistible popularity of the mouth-watering dish, it is vilified enough in Indian society that it can effectively change public perception during a trial. In the end, Ajmal Kasab was declared a terrorist on the basis of a blurred picture claimed to have been taken during the Mumbai terror attacks.

Indians still love Biryani but with the rise of the right-wing Hindu nationalist Bharatiya Janata Party (BJP), things have changed intensely. BJP demonized the food to an extent that now it seems to be a crime to serve or eat Biryani. During the recent electoral debate, Yogi Adityanath, a BJP chief minister accused his political rival Arvind Kejriwal, of serving Biryani to the demonstrators protesting the controversial Citizenship Amendment Bill (CAB), as if distributing and eating Biryani is a crime. According to a *Guardian* article, Adityanath said that thousands of women protesting against the bill are terrorists and they should be "fed with bullets not Biryani."

Before discussing the nitty-gritties of the Indian political rhetoric against Biryani, this question must be answered: Why did an all-time favourite dish which earned international fame become a villain in the polarizing political scenario? The answer is simple: Because Biryani is considered a Muslim dish. Indian politics is dominated by Hindu nationalists who secure votes through hate speech against minorities, specifically Muslims. Biryani in Indian politics represents India's largest minority: i.e. 17.2 million Muslims. BJP Hindu nationalist ideology is based on minority hate. Minorities are hated and so is the dish associated with them. According to the Hindu nationalist ideology (Hindutva), everything Muslim is a threat to India. Biryani threatens Hindu nationalists as a cultural representation of the enemy.

A disclaimer: Hindutva and Hinduism are not the same. Hindutva is a hate- based ideology merely developed around the 1920s. On the other hand, Hinduism is one of the most ancient faiths which has over a thousand years of history of coexistence with other religions. The Hindu nationalists' hatred towards minorities has not stopped at Biryani bashing. According to a 2017 *The Atlantic* article, more than two dozen Muslims and Dalits have been publicly lynched since the BJP assumed power in 2014. After their electoral victory, the government unofficially approved and condoned these tens of thousands of vigilante groups across India to monitor the violation of the ban on beef consumption and cow slaughter as cows are sacred in Hinduism. These Gau-Raksha or cow protection groups used the beef ban to justify their attacks on innocent men in public with impunity. The rights group says that the ban on beef provides the license for public lynchings often based on fake accusations. Yale scholar Radha Sarkar has argued in her 2016 paper that the bans on beef "tacitly legitimize vigilante activity" and violence by cow vigilantes. According to a report by *The Economic Times of India*, in 2016, Shashi Tharoor, the Oxford-educated prolific writer and Indian parliamentarian quoted his Bangladeshi friend to contend that a "cow is safer in India than a Muslim" suggesting "growing intolerance" in the country.

Ironically, India is the larger exporter of beef in the world, earning four billion dollars annually from bovine trade. I believe it is not the beef that is behind the lynchings but a hatred of Muslims and Dalits, both vulnerable minorities in India. According to a report by *Hindustan Times*, in February 2020, a Muslim farmer in West Bengal was lynched and later strangled to death by five men inside his home because his son damaged the mobile phone of his neighbour. In May 2020, a thirty-year-old Muslim man was beaten to death by a crowd on the accusation of stealing a goat. While the NDTV's (mainstream Indian media group) report mentioned no claimant of the goat stealing, two separate cases were filed by police: one against the lynched victim for stealing and one against the attackers. Those indicted in public lynchings are seldom convicted. Supriya Nair, a Mumbai based journalist writes, "In the aftermath of these beef lynchings, police investigations have moved glacially; victims' families are sometimes threatened with counter-charges of cow slaughter; political condemnation has been absent or lukewarm, if not outright tendentious." After four years of impunity, in July 2018, Indian Supreme Court finally condemned lynching: "horrendous acts of mobocracy cannot be tolerated and cannot be allowed to become a new norm."

But the hatred doesn't stop at lynchings. Hindutva ideology is pushing India towards neo-Fascism and Nazism, and extermination of the Indian Muslims. There are organizations in Sangh Parivar that are publicly advocating forced conversion of Non-Hindu subjects to Hinduism. About a century ago, Hindutva organizations like Shudhi (a Sanskrit word meaning purification) publicly advocated that only Hindus have a right to live in India and Non-Hindus can live in India if and only if they convert to Hinduism. Now they are in power to make their dream a reality. According to an article published in *The*

Washington Post in 2017, Yogi Adityanath, the chief minister of India's largest state Uttar Pradesh, promised people a Muslim-free India in his election campaign. What he promises is extermination and the final solution. Notably, Amnesty International India asked him to publicly withdraw his inflammatory statements against Muslims and other minorities. The Right group demand went unheard.

Muslims, an already vulnerable minority, which forms about fifteen percent of India's 1.3 billion people, were increasingly marginalised since independence. As London University researcher Rochana Bajpai portrays the picture of systematic discrimination towards the Muslim minority in her 2017 paper: "In education, Muslims are under-represented at all levels, with outcomes declining as we move up the education ladder. These exclusions are reinforced by high levels of poverty, illiteracy, poor access to health amenities and segregated housing. In government employment, Muslim share is less than half their share of the population of the country. This, combined with low shares in private sector employment, make Muslims 'the most deprived minority in the labour market.'"

Since the Hindu nationalists' rise in power, this systematic discrimination has escalated to an extent that Indian intellectuals are talking about holocaust and genocide. Talking to the German newspaper *Der Spiegel*, Arundhati Roy, one of the most popular Indian fiction writers and political activists of international fame, said that BJP is exploiting the COVID-19 epidemic to suppress Muslims in the same way as Nazis used Typhus against the Jews, and that "the situation is approaching genocidal."

Recent anti-Muslim pogroms in Delhi are seen as the Kristallnacht equivalent of India by regional geopolitical experts who are closely monitoring the situation as Patrick Cockburn of *The Independent* writes, "There are some grim parallels between *Kristallnacht* in Germany in 1938 and Delhi today." Meanwhile, US President Donald Trump was eating Biryani in the Raj Bhawan, the official residence of the Indian prime minister. During Trump's visit, Hindu nationalist mobs were allowed to attack Muslim neighbourhoods, burn their houses, shops, and even mosques. While the Indian government calls them communal riots, police and the government machinery always take the side of the Hindu nationalists as Bajpai argues: "in the frequent incidents of inter-community violence across the country, the collusion of the police with anti-Muslim mobs has been a consistent pattern, leading to much greater losses of Muslim lives and property in riots." Indian intellectuals and academics are constantly warning that these pogroms dubbed communal riots are an early stage genocide. "A pogrom, which some might insist is nothing more than an ordinary riot, can quite easily turn into genocide," writes Samantak Das, professor of comparative literature at Jadavpur University, India. Nazism is not an unfamiliar concept to Hindutva, the ideology of Hindu nationalists. V. D. Savarkar, the man who laid the ideological foundations of Hindutva, was a great admirer of Hitler and his policy of pogroms against the Jews. In 1923, he describes Hindutva, as an ideology based on three essential pillars: a common nation (Rashtra), a common race (Jati), and a common culture or civilization (Sanskriti). Hindutva has stark similarities with the Nazi ideology which is based on ein volk (one people), ein reich (one nation), ein Fuhrer (one leader).

And yet... Since antiquity, India has been a diverse mix of people who believe in different religions, speak different languages, and practice a variety of colourful cultures. The deserts of Rajhastan, the plains of Punjab, the mountainous regions of Simla, and coastal regions of Southern India each have their own colours, smells, and flavours but they are part of one single mosaic called India. The same is true for a diverse mix of religions, races, and ethnicities. They are like a hot plate of Biryani with rice of different colours, a blend of exotic spices, meat, and irresistible aroma. Each ingredient has its own unique flavour, fragrance, and colour but what makes them one of the most demanded continental cuisines is their coexistence.

I still serve Biryani to family and friends during camping trips in the Canadian Rockies, and my ageing parents still feel nostalgia for the tolerant India they experienced growing up. They tell us the stories of their childhood in Jodhpur, Rajasthan, and Bhopal, Madhya Pradesh. While my mother's ancestors arrived in India centuries ago from Arabia, my father's Hindu-born ancestors embraced Islamic faith by their own will. Amid fears of Hindutva domination and discrimination in an independent India, families of both had to migrate to Pakistan after 1947.

Biryani and pluralism are both endangered in India. If pluralism is threatened, the existence of Indian society is threatened; India's diversity is not a threat. It is what makes it great.

Resolviendo
Ana Ruiz Aguirre

Everyone has the right to a standard of living adequate for the health and well-being of himself and of his family, including food, clothing, housing and medical care and necessary social services, and the right to security in the event of unemployment, sickness, disability, widowhood, old age or other lack of livelihood in circumstances beyond his control.

—Universal Declaration of Human Rights (1948)

Provided my grandmother managed to resolver the necessary ingredients, the mornings always started with café con leche and toasted bread with butter churned by my grandfather by hand in our backyard. The verb resolver means to solve, but in Cuba it is also the word of choice to indicate any activity related to procuring goods on the black market.

Food was declared a human right by the United Nations (UN) in the Universal Declaration of Human Rights of 1948. Not that it matters very much. Some countries still produce excess food and discard it to maintain market prices or comply with aesthetic export requirements, while other countries, like Cuba, struggle to provide its citizens with this basic need. As an immigrant, I've experienced deep conflicts moving between the geopolitical lieux de mémoire of these two extremes. This process forces me to see food as nourishment, and also as a political tool and cultural signifier which can sometimes reinforce social hierarchies, economic systems, and community ties.

    I grew up in Cuba during the Special Period, a term euphemistically utilized to designate the 1990s, a decade when the country experienced severe food shortages. A 1997 report by the World Health Organization (WHO) declared the situation a direct result of the ongoing trade embargo imposed by the US against Cuba since 1962, sharply restricting the sale of food to the island after 1992, taking advantage of the collapse of the Soviet Union (Cuba's main trading partner), and encouraging social unrest in the country. These food shortages, continues the report, caused devastating damage to the Cuban population, including an outbreak of neuropathy numbering in the tens of thousands. This policy continued until 2002, when the Clinton administration caved in to pressure exerted by US agricultural producers, allowing limited food sales to the island, while also acquiescing to the Cuban-American lobby that all payments would have to be made in cash.

    During this time, finding food in Cuba as a private citizen was a challenge. Shortages breed corruption, and every level within the national food distribution system was susceptible to widespread theft. The government distributed a basic food package to each household at cost, containing staples like rice, beans, bread, oil, and sugar. However, this subsidized food package was insufficient to cover nutritional needs and Cubans promptly turned to a flourishing black market to find food. The black market, el mercado negro, was conspicuous; all you needed was enough money to pay the inflated prices.

    In Santiago de Cuba, my grandmother would buy European cheeses stolen from Spanish hotel chains operating in the city from a skinny blond man who brought big blocks of Spanish Manchego and Dutch Gouda to our home. She bought milk from farmers who brought it to the city fresh from the countryside, deviated from the quota they were required to sell to the government for national distribution. Everything was acquired similarly: fruits, spices, meats, canned goods, preserves, flour, and even coffee. In this market consumers were not overly selective; they had to buy whatever was available at the time. Coffee produced in the nearby mountain ranges was a particular item abuela always needed to resolver. Cuban coffee is strong, thick, and sweet, with the majority of it produced 100km away from where I was born. Like every Cuban I know, I am committed to importing the maximum amount of coffee allowed by the CBSA every time I return to Edmonton from Cuba, so I can replicate the national tradition of café con leche in the mornings.

Abuela started making lunch as soon as breakfast ended, if not the day before. Lunch was always the heaviest meal of the day, and it consisted mostly of Galician food. Her father, my great-grandfather, migrated to Cuba from Lugo, Galicia, in the early 20th century, exercising the famous dictum by fellow Galician Alfonso Daniel Rodríguez Castelao who affirmed Galicians migrated instead of protesting: el gallego no protesta, emigra. Almost a century later, I tasted Galicia in the tropics through empanadas gallegas, callos con garbanzo, and mariscadas. The empanadas were and continue to be my favourite; a mix of fresh tuna and olives I indefatigably attempt to replicate unsuccessfully. Food that tastes of a place.

At dinner time, Galicia gave way to Africa. We ate accra or frituritas de malanga—fritters made from ground malanga also popular in Haiti—and fried plantains accompanied by rice and beans, the most popular Cuban dish of all time. For special family occasions, my grandmother would make ensalada de pollo, a labour-intensive Cuban dish from the central province of Ciego de Ávila containing finely chopped chicken, potatoes, and pineapples. During popular celebrations, the entire block would gather around a large cauldron placed in the middle of the street to make ajiaco. Concocting this soup entailed an exercise in community building; each person contributed whatever ingredient they could: pig heads, corn cobs, and sacks full of tubers were thrown unceremoniously in the pot as Cuban music blasted and everyone drank dark, aged rum.

Ajiaco is special. Cuban ethnologist Fernando Ortiz famously developed the concept of ajiaco as a metaphor for Cuba's national identity in his book *Contrapunteo cubano del tabaco y el azúcar*, first published in 1940. In it, Ortiz developed an alternative to the concept of acculturation or "melting pot" espoused by the United States at the time. In his view, Cuba experienced a transculturation process initiated with colonization which entailed complex transmutations of culture and ongoing national exchanges and tensions between national cultural groups, but never dissolution into one singular, monolithic culture. Each ingredient in the nation, he thought, kept its own taste while contributing to the collective.

Like ajiaco, Ortiz saw Cuba as a communal pot containing all sorts of ever-changing ingredients. His interpretation is particularly pertinent since ajiaco is one of the few remnants in contemporary Cuban cuisine of the Taíno, the Indigenous peoples from the northern Caribbean who welcomed Colombus upon arrival to Cuban shores in 1492 and were exterminated shortly after. The genocide of the Taíno in Cuba acted as a catalyst for the introduction of African cuisine on the island, as Spaniards engaged in slave trade to find replacement labour. A significant number of the men and women brought through the slave trade to Cuba came from the ancient Yoruba Oyo Empire which spanned territories in today's Benin and Nigeria. Taro, malanga, and plantains, staples in Cuban contemporary food, were brought with them in the ships and eventually made their way to the colonizers' tables, as families and cultural groups were kept together in the haciendas and allowed to maintain their practices under the belief that doing so increased their productivity. Today, Yoruba culture continues to run deep in Cuba, expressed in everyday language, predominant religious practices, and food including the delicious fufú, a popular mix of mashed plantains with palm tree oil.

When I moved to Edmonton in 2006, I quickly learned there would be no ajiaco unless I made it, and my entire culinary universe collapsed with that realization. Ever the family matriarch, abuela did not allow any other family members in the kitchen. She ruled over her domain with the occasional help of Mari, her domestic assistant for decades, who was the only living soul who could set foot in her kitchen with relative impunity. As a result, neither my mother nor I had any cooking skills whatsoever when we moved north, and during our learning process we had to unwillingly rely on the Canadian staples my stepfather cooked. In Edmonton the supermarkets were full of unfamiliar, processed products which I did not recognize as food. Processed foods were rare in Cuba as a result of the trade embargo, as were agricultural chemicals and technology, which meant the overwhelming majority of the food I could access growing up was locally grown and organic. In Edmonton, produce tasted different, more muted; the milk jugs had percentages printed on the labels.

My mother and I ventured into this new food milieu armed with two cookbooks and hand-written recipes abuela gave us; a cultural patrimony of sorts. Both books are Cuban classics: a 1954 edition of Maria Teresa Cotta de Cal's *Comidas criollas en ollas de presión*, and a 1959 edition of Nitza Villapol's classic *Cocina al minuto*, a book which every Cuban living on the island or in the diaspora knows very well and treasures. We diligently scoured small produce shops around 118th Avenue and other underprivileged communities for key ingredients like the right type of malanga to make frituritas. We also looked for Cuban food restaurants but only found two, both of them already out of business.

In Edmonton, I've experienced the overwhelming opinion that Cuban food is tasteless, bland, and overall, not very good, a position I theorize is justified by the tendency of Edmontonians as a collective to visit Cuban all-inclusive resorts almost exclusively. Tourist resorts, as I mentioned earlier, are the source of much of the food available in the Cuban black market: food is stolen from the hotels and sold to private businesses and Cuban families in the cities, leaving Edmontonians and other foreigners to holiday with the scraps. I find there is a poetic justice in it all, a sort of unconscious resistance to the neo-colonization implicit in contemporary tourism practices and the poverty porn craved, and consumed by many Canadians who visit Cuba.

Despite it all, I firmly believe everyone should resolver ajiaco as a culinary and collective event. Especially in places like Edmonton, where half of the population was born elsewhere. The metaphor of society as a soup with distinct, changing ingredients that form a delicious collective should be the goal we strive to accomplish as a community. To inspire you, here is an ajiaco recipe you can make on your own, although I find it tastes better when cooked by a group having fun and taking the ingredient list as a suggestion, of course with Cuban music blasting and everyone drinking dark, aged rum.

Ajiaco

Ingredients

1kg	spare ribs
100g	cassava
100g	yams
100g	sweet potatoes
100g	pumpkin
2 cobs	fresh corn
1	plantain
30g	tomato paste
30g	chopped onions
30g	chopped garlic
50ml	olive oil
	salt

Instructions

1. Set a large pot of water to boil. Separate the spare ribs and then tip them into the boiling water. Allow to cook for 1 hour on low heat.

2. Peel the cassava, yams, sweet potatoes, and pumpkin. Dice the tubers and pumpkin coarsely. Shuck the corn cobs, rinse and cut into disks. Keep the plantain separate.

3. Tip the meat, yams, sweet potatoes, cassava, pumpkin, and corn into the stock. Bring to a boil.

4. Sauté the chopped garlic and onions in hot oil for 5 minutes until golden. Add them to the pot. Then stir in the tomato paste and salt, and allow to cook for 30 to 40 minutes.

5. Cut the plantain into disks and fry for 5 minutes in the hot oil. Add to the soup immediately prior to serving, piping hot, in a soup tureen.

Resolviendo

Culinary Heritage

Anna Marie Sewell (*Canada*)
Five Recipes

Marco Melfi (*Italy-Canada*)
Empty Mason Jars

Five Recipes

Anna Marie Sewell

We are built of the foods of our ancestors. From my father's side, Anishinaabe and Mi'gmaq. On my distaff side, Polish peasantry. From both sides, I learned kitchen values, and relationships with food beyond the food court. In my own right, I've travelled, worked, learned, and collected new connections to cuisine and culture.

Let's begin with Polish food.

1 Staff of Life

This recipe begins in Poland, in 1928, when my grandparents decided it was time to leave, before martial law and then the Communist bloc overtook their traditional home.

Their journey to Canada took months, if you begin with Grandma and four little children, the youngest a baby in her arms, rushing out the back door with all they'd gathered for the journey. Grandpa stayed behind, barring the door against the soldiers who'd taken to robbing anyone whom they'd discovered saving up to emigrate. He caught up, by the time they sailed for Halifax, six people whose name had been changed to Sawchuk, along with Grandpa's sisters and their husbands. From Pier 21 they went on to Alberta, to homestead land in the South Peace country. It was a world away from the settled, prosperous village farms of Bialy Podlaska.

What can you carry that far? Seeds and recipes, strength and faith in the time-tested alchemy. Turn the furrow, plant the crop, tend the fields, and grind the grain. Save back the best seed to begin again.

Grandma's children ground grain by hand in the evenings, for her to bake bread.

My mother baked twice a week, for her family of eight-plus-fosterlings. In her time, a flour bin filled by fifty-pound bags brought home from town. In my time, small bags, small batches, time to experiment with flax, grated apple, spices, braided shapes. Turn and push, turn and punch, knuckles kneading. I spin the bowl slowly, to let the dough know, as my mother taught me, the wishes in my heart and mind for prosperity for all my relations. She'd say your prayer, like the dough, rises on God's say-so.

2   Cabbage Rolls

Grandma's farmhouse always had a crock of sauerkraut in the cool front hall. She made cabbage rolls with pork. Mom switched to ground beef, mixed with moose in season, as my eldest brother was allergic to pork.

Mom's rectangular roast pans full of cabbage rolls filled the oven on Christmas Eve. Back when Dad still attended church, we'd all go to Midnight Mass, and drive home singing, squabbling, nodding off. Once home, Mom would open a roaster, and everyone could have a cabbage roll or two before bed.

Christmas itself was a one-meal day, the feast timed for early afternoon. For breakfast in the meanwhile? Cabbage rolls, of course, as many as we wanted. However hungry we were, however many guests filled the house, there were always plenty of cabbage rolls for dinner.

When my first sister wed, our oldest aunt came out from BC to help cook for the reception. We all gathered at my sister's townhouse the night before the wedding, camping out in the living room after decorating the north Edmonton community league hall.

I remember waking at 3:00 am to the sound of Aunty giggling, 'Come on, Sister,' as they nimbly scampered through the maze of sleepers, off to fire up the ovens and start their cabbage rolls. Mom was already in her late fifties, Aunty over seventy, but they whispered and capered like the girls they'd always carried in their hearts.

I wed late. Aunty, in her nineties, was too frail to travel out from BC. Mom herself was eighty-two, and had just completed two years of cancer treatment. She'd lived with us through those years, gardening with me, walking to church, and giving my daughter the gifts of inter- generational connection. At school 'heritage days' my daughter proudly showed off the cabbage rolls her grandma had let her help roll; Grandma taught her to bake, play cribbage, keep your own counsel. Then Grandma went home to the Peace Country.

And in 2015, we came into some money, an inheritance from my long-dead father. So we threw a wedding. After sixteen years together, it certainly wasn't following tradition of either of our families. We didn't have a cake. We had a wedding haggis. A father and son team of vegan cooks made most of the rest of our feast. But pride of place? Cabbage rolls, of course.

My mother came down to the city and turned my kitchen into a factory. She made 350 cabbage rolls before the element in my oven burnt out. And we feasted.

Mom left this world in 2017. I carry the recipe as memory, never written. Grandma Sawchuk was illiterate. It was her hands that knew. My mother wrote many things, but cabbage rolls? That recipe is handed down.

3 Great Chieftain o' the Puddin' Race!

I was already over thirty when my life partner walked up to me at a poetry reading and told me I was wrong about Robbie Burns, whom he took it I was critiquing in verse. I do believe my first words to him were, 'Who the hell are you?' Intrigued and undaunted, he persisted, inviting me to a haggis dinner with his friends.

Over the years, Robbie Burns Night has become our yearly tradition; we fill our house with friends and food, music and verse, and toast the Bard of Scotland with my husband's acclaimed declamation of Address to a Haggis.

It is his grandmother who was Scottish, her clan tartan he

wears. When first we met, he'd barely memorized the Address, and amused party guests by appearing in a plaid bathrobe to declaim. Then his best friends pooled their money and bought him a bespoke formal kilt of his own, which he wears at all formal occasions.

Yes, he was wed in it. And rented matching kilts and jackets for his groomsmen, who rode to our outdoor ceremony on bikes, through the park, ringing their bells as they came.

These days, our January ritual includes friends playing Renaissance recorders, a man with a claymore, occasional youth dancers, and a full house of people clapping and roaring at the poem's climax: 'Gi 'er a Haggis!'

But do we have a haggis recipe of our own? Not as such. There have been years when, through family connections, we've obtained sheep's stomachs. Then, we gleefully ground up the requisite organ meat, mixed it with oatmeal and onion and pepper, stuffed the stomachs and boiled our own haggis from scratch.

The first year we tried it, we used the stomachs whole, ignorant of how far they can stretch, how they might bloat… I recall opening the mighty stockpot to check on our lumpy experiment, and exclaiming in horror, for we appeared to be cooking Dolly Parton. We've learned. And, with the advent of halal butchers and the shift in markets here for meat, we can now buy stomach in several markets around town. We know we can make our own if we have to. But we also know a really good specialty shop in south Edmonton, a small business that specializes in haggis.

So, we support them, as they carry forward the tradition. Their freezers are well stocked, year-round. Come January, pride of place goes to ranks of cooked, frozen haggises, ready to come home and be lauded as the Bard first named them, as Great Chieftains o' the Puddin' Race.

4   Swiss Steak

I grew up on farms in northern Alberta, my mother's homeland. She married an army man, and they lived on bases for the first few years. When children arrived, she convinced him that the farm life would provide better for a large family. So, a musician and gunnery sergeant, raised on an Ontario reservation, my father followed her back to her Peace Country. He used his army pension to buy some land and set out to learn how to farm.

A bit unusually for that time and place, my dad was openly, proudly Ojibway (nowadays, the fashion is to call us Anishinaabe, but Dad was Ojibway). My mom told well-meaning folks, who suggested that she say he was French, just exactly what to do with what was *their* problem—not hers, and not to be foisted upon her children. She was Polish, and her patriarchal traditions accorded with Canadian government reckoning. Though I've come to see how very Polish-Canadian are many traditions I hold, I was raised claiming that part of my identity that others would have rather seen hidden.

So, I knew I was an 'Indian.' And the prejudices of small-town Alberta concerning Indians, and extended as well to 'dirty Halfbreeds,' were the wind against which I learned to walk. But what did it mean to be Ojibway, in Cree country? My dad went to Church schools, in English. It was only the odd Ojibway expression and turn of phrase that persisted, the occasional bursts of accent.

As for food? Mom told me, in the years when she lived in my city home, that in fact, Dad had been the household cook; when they married, she didn't know how. By the time I was old enough to notice, Dad would only preside over the occasional stew, or his specialty, Swiss Steak, or rather, what you make when you have plenty of moose meat to cook.

Dad would take the biggest of our fleet of cast iron pans, put in a bit of fat—lard, tallow, cooking oil, whatever was handiest—and cut in an onion to brown. Then, fill the pan with steak to sear on one side, whilst opening a big can of tomatoes with their juice to just cover the steaks. Put on the lid, wait, and keep smelling. When the time is right, turn the steaks. Once only. Cook some more. You'll know when they're done right, for that tough old moose will be tender.

I remember him sitting in his chair, in his corner of the farmhouse kitchen, with his big mug of tea, coaching me through the process. The only part I didn't enjoy was cutting the canned tomatoes, sticking the mid-sized sharp knife into the can and pressing them until they broke. The other option was to chop them in the pan. Food processors never figured into it. He knew what he knew.

I would occasionally try to cajole him into letting me use a can of tomato paste, but he'd remind me, those were for cabbage rolls. So, I'd hack those tomatoes. Now, I grow my own. With only a small household, I have enough for sauces.

I am a city person now, and I don't hunt. I have friends who do, and who will, on occasion, bring me wild meat as a treat. But my Swiss Steak is usually ossobuco, a nice fat cut of beef shank with the bone in—Dad loved marrow, too, and it is the cheap cut at the local Italian grocery. I open my home-canned tomato sauce—the tomatoes chopped raw, the skins kept in for nostalgia—and while it simmers, I look at the patterns of ground pepper on the surface, and think of how our lives are tiny, mobile, moments of joy.

5 Hainan Chicken, by way of Dim Sum

I moved to Edmonton in 1985. My father came down on the air ambulance, and died in an operating room on the day I first worked at a city job. Through the lean student years that followed, my Mom and younger siblings kept the farm alive. Mom brought farm produce down in care packages. For some years, she raised Muscovy ducks, and I learned to cook those. She did what she could, and I am eternally grateful. But I'd have never gone hungry anyway.

My best friends in school were both daughters of Chinese immigrants. After high school, they moved to an urban setting where their families had standing connections. So, when I arrived, when my sister's fiancé, then my father, then my brother, died young, they carried me through, without fuss. They were my guides to all the best our city had to offer from the rich heritage of Chinese cuisine.

For all my student years, I was included in family Dim Sums, invited to New Year's feasts, and introduced to many incredible delicacies both rare and workaday. Chinatown in the 80s was still vibrant with sidewalk vendors, curio shops full of cheap and useful housewares, and restaurants legendary for their tales of Triad intrigues and mysterious back ways. I felt I'd arrived at the very door of the wide world, drinking tea with my beloved friends, letting the language flow over my head. They taught me Dim Sum Cantonese, enough to take a turn ordering once in a while, and that was plenty.

In 1997, after years of working abroad, I returned to

Edmonton. One day, I took a walk in Chinatown, and followed my nose into a little restaurant that looked and smelled like all those memories. I'd never been to this particular restaurant, but it felt like a proper homecoming. In a burst of glee, I ordered something I'd never tried. And so an addiction was born. For years, I'd go alone to this little place, my secret restaurant, and after a while, they didn't even ask, just grinned and brought me the Hainan. Why didn't I bring my girlfriends there? Why does anyone need to make their own grown-up relationship with family things? This was my choice, my proof that I'd learned well from the families who carried me through the lean young years. To bring them might be an unseemly show-off move. I knew how to be a regular in Chinatown.

By and by, I brought my life partner. When our daughter was born, he carried her there for the first time, tucked up in a carrier on his belly. The proprietors beamed and cooed over her. And until they sold out a few years back, Hainan Chicken was a regular part of my girl's diet. The deaf waitress, now retired, will still wave at me in Chinatown, still gesturing animatedly, asking how tall my daughter is. I'll sign back, she'll sigh and sign about all those chicken dinners.

And in my own kitchen, I'll chop garlic, ginger, green onion; mix them in a bowl with sesame oil and vinegar while the chicken legs poach in the saucepan. Then I'll pour in the sauce, to finish with the chicken while the rice with its powdered galangal steams out.

If I'm feeling lazy, I'll buy a pack of pre-made Hainan Chicken sauce and use that instead. I'm not fussy. It's not how the restaurant made it, but it tastes like home, and like all the recipes I claim, I've made it my own.

Empty Mason Jars — Marco Melfi

My relationship to food changed when I moved to Edmonton in my mid-twenties. I no longer had access to the bounty of my Nonna's pizza, veal cutlets sliced and breaded to perfection or her classic pizzelle. While Edmonton had an array of local, independent grocery stores and farmers' markets, I hesitated to trust the many brands of tomato sauce when, to that point, I had only known homemade. This presented the perfect opportunity to finally follow the example of my family, to replicate my Nonna's recipe, and stock my cupboards with my very own sauce.

The journey included a trip to the Italian Centre on a quest to locate the ripest Roma tomatoes. I transformed the tiny apartment I lived in with my wife into a sauce assembly line. I filled the dozen Mason jars with a poppy red paste that reminded me of the shelves in my Nonna's cellar. Once I tightened the last lid, I proudly posted evidence of my effort on Instagram. My Nonna seemed impressed when I told her over the phone. I had joined everyone in my family who had all jarred sauce. The accomplishment and connection to a family craft contributed to my sense of what it meant to be Italian-Canadian.

I assumed I would refill the jars and improve on that initial batch. However, the jars sat empty the next season and the season after that. They were bubble wrapped, moved from our apartment to our new house and last used as drinking glasses. A guilt accompanied each year that passed yet my interest to jar sauce again had waned. The multi-step process was one factor: there was the patience needed to peel the skins off blanched tomatoes, strain them once blended, and all that boiling and sanitizing. Making sauce as I needed it—whether quick on a weeknight or a slow simmer on a Sunday—suited me better. Plus, beyond my job, hanging out with my wife, my friends, or playing soccer I dedicated a lot of time to writing and participating in Edmonton's poetry and literary community. The longer the jars stayed empty the more I worried about letting my family down and what it meant to my identity. Eventually, I donated the Mason jars to Goodwill.

From academic scholarship to personal recollections, the centrality of food to the Italian immigrant sense of identity and community is well documented. Jim Zucchero, in *Risotto and Resistance: In the Shadow of the Italian Kitchen*, highlights the influence food can have on identity. He describes how food provides rich cultural insights both because we consume it for daily sustenance as well as associate it with celebration. Food's multisensory nature—that combination of how a dish looks, smells, tastes, or where we eat it and with whom—can have a powerful effect on us. Food delights, triggers memories, impacts how we see ourselves, and how we relate to others. In Jessica Kluthe's book, *Rosina, the Midwife*, a story about her family's migration from Calabria to Edmonton, references to food are woven throughout to underscore the relationship between family and sense of self. The kitchen is a recurring setting to symbolize that relationship. Kluthe shows this is where her sister "collected all of Nanni's secrets over pound cakes, and all the stories about Calabria—the Old Country—while picking peas or peeling apples." In another passage, Kluthe describes the time she savoured at her grandparents' house: "I took small bites of my breakfast and sipped my pulpy orange juice because I wanted to stay, seated there, in the middle of it all." Both Zucchero and Kluthe help to highlight my own relationship with food and identity.

Born to parents who emigrated from Molise and Sicily, I have had Italian food and the eventful times squeezed into kitchens as a positive constant in my life. These positive associations span my earliest memories devouring Nutella sandwiches after school to the excitement today for special occasions and special dishes: like "Pasta with the Hands" for La Festa di San Giuseppe or my Nonna's white lasagna for Christmas. That white lasagna is a family favourite not just for its brothy layers filled with capon, but in recognition of the level of effort to make it: sheets as thin as tissue paper, veal meatballs rolled smaller than marbles, and the broth boiled more by alchemy than recipe. This combination of food, gathering, and the appreciation for homemade dishes is wrapped up in my sense of self.

The kitchen also represents the place I developed a special bond with my grandparents; where I spent countless lunch hours at their downtown Hamilton home. I recall these visits fondly because of my grandparents' gift for storytelling. Their stories ranged from their life in Italy, their experiences during World War II, their emigration, or how they adapted to living in Canada. Food was a regular theme. I could picture my grandmother as a young girl trekking to town with milk from her farm or the bread baked in the murky hours between night and day. Or their families' modest meals of simple pastas because meat was expensive and only for occasions. The vivid details of what they ate or the scenes and relatives they were with have prompted me to write many of these stories down. I admired the endless knowledge and skills, imparted to them, and honed in Molise, that transferred to their life in Canada. How decades after they immigrated in the 1950s, they still had these practices.

This background provided me with a greater appreciation for how proud they were of the tomatoes, zucchini, and eggplants they grew in their garden in Hamilton; the boxes upon boxes of pears and apples they picked; the vegetables they canned, jarred, and froze to sustain them throughout the year; or the wine my grandfather always preferred from grapes he pressed himself. It was inspirational and characterized a key trait I ascribed to being Italian-Canadian: pride in what they grew and made and how it tied back to where they came from.

I half expected to one day adopt many of these practices. I believed it would contribute to my identity and was necessary to honour my grandparents' work ethic and example. The worry I had with those empty Mason jars included losing that connection between who I was and where I had come from. However, the worry and the expectations that weighed on me were self-inflicted. My grandparents never required me to follow their lead. Even now during long-distance calls with my Nonna, we'll talk about the last feast day, which dishes were had, or how our gardens are progressing. But how much I've made from scratch or what I've canned never comes up. My connection to my roots is much deeper than the competency I demonstrate with my homemade habits. Donating the jars allowed me to release the pressure I placed on myself and allowed me to refocus on what I was creating.

While I've mastered pasta with clams or frying up a batch of zucchini chips and am slowly gaining more confidence with a small garden plot, I know cooking and homemade practices are not innate. They take interest, work, and time. I spend more of mine filling notebooks with the anecdotes that accompany the recipes from my grandparents. I am more likely to co-opt the alliterative list of ingredients or the rich sights, smells, sounds, and textures found in a kitchen and bring them into my writing. I've come to recognize I earn more joy channeling my time and interest here.

My relationship to food remains important to me. The scene from Kluthe's book reminded me of my own family, especially my grandparents, and the kitchen as an influential setting. Initially, I thought those experiences would serve to make me as stellar a DIYer as my grandparents. Instead, food and those memories serve as fruitful sources I love to draw on for my poetry. I've embraced my own way to honour my grandparents, their example, and I'll keep writing until I've cooked something just right.

Culinary Nostalgia

Shimelis Gebremichael (*Ethiopia*)
Missing the Beloved Injera

Leilei Chen (*China*)
Food Ties

Shimelis Gebremichael
Missing the Beloved Injera

The Canadian version of Ethiopian food with all its smells, colours, and grace was so surprising. "Well, the food looks the same as what you know back home, but the taste is definitely different!" My friend had read my mind. Following my life-changing farewell in Addis Ababa back in 2013, my Edmonton welcome was festooned with laughter and a heartwarming banquet from my wife and her friends. Observing the food, I compared notes to the one I left back home. I specially recall tiibs beef cut into small chunks and sautéed in butter or oil with onions, garlic, hot pepper, and rosemary, as well as kitfo, a ground raw beef that's been mixed with kibbe [spiced clarified butter]. You could imagine how I voraciously ate after an over twenty hours' flight. That's where I got stuck, stopped chewing in the middle of my dining recalling the saying, "all that glitters is not gold." Judging the food by its cover, I had a hard time disguising my disappointment. Nothing I tasted was like what I knew back home.

Ethiopia, with its over eighty ethnicities, has an astonishing variety of foods and flavours. The Ethiopian dining rituals are unforgettable. The taste of the food is accompanied by careful procedures, leaving you with a gratification close to that of love and affection, of amplified satiety after calming hunger pangs. It all starts with Injera. Our Ethiopian staple consists of a flat bread served with different sauces. Westerners describe it as a foamy pancake. It has a rather sour taste resulting from the dough being fermented for a few days prior to baking. We eat Injera alongside a stew called wot, which comes in two generic forms: the hot sauce (red stew), flavoured with berbere (ground chilli), onions, and garlic and, aalicha wot (yellow stew), onions and garlic, with no berbere. On non-fasting days, wot is usually made with meat such as lamb (beg), goat (fiyel), beef (bere), and fish (asa). Siga tiibs (meat fried with pepper), kitfo (spicy raw or lightly cooked mincemeat), and gulash (a mild spicy stew) are some of the spices served with Injera. Ethiopian immigrants tend to say: "le injera biye tesededkugn" [I left my home country looking for Injera], which could be translated to 'seeking my bread and butter' in the Anglophonic context.

Normally, authentic Ethiopian Injera is very sour, according to our mothers, because of the special properties of yeast in it. The real Injera is made with teff, a tiny, round grain that flourishes in the highlands of Ethiopia. In Edmonton, Injera could either be bought for $5.00 from convenience stores, with five pieces in a plastic bag, or could be made at home. Ethiopians can't survive without it for a week if not for three days.

The last Injera I savoured before I arrived in Edmonton was decorated with different vegan and meat sauces. The dish looks like the incredible countryside summer landscapes of Ethiopia that you mainly observe at the onset of September, the beginning of the Ethiopian Year, with its yellows, greens, and blazing reds. That ornate meal does not only evoke the landscapes of Ethiopia; it also imprints them in the souls of its citizens.

In the face of this visually appealing yet flavourless spread, I kept my true opinion to myself; my culture and their relentless efforts in a new environment made me appreciate them even more. "Wow! The food is so delicious, Thank you so much!" I complimented my hosts' efforts as I made eye contact with my wife whom I had missed deeply in our years of separation. My wife smiled warmly at me.

My first impression about the Ethiopian food I tasted here in Edmonton was the scarcity of the main ingredient, teff, and the addition of grains foreign to Ethiopian cuisine, like rice, easily accessible in Canada's grocery shops. I wished the festivities and my honeymoon reunion would continue for days. However, in no time, everyone dispersed, including my wife. They had jobs to go to and bills to pay. Like the ingredient teff, time is in abundance in Ethiopia yet so precious in Canada; every hour and minute counts.

"Our lord Jesus Christ was born in a manger in Bethlehem," the priest kept on preaching, my heart and mind instead escaping straight to the smell in the basement. We only have brief moments together at our church on Sundays during prayers and dining, especially on holidays. In the gatherings of our Orthodox Tewahido Church (EOTC), food is the central element as there is a strong belief that it creates an enduring bond between people. Unlike in the Western tradition, our church celebrates Christmas fourteen days after the European Christmas, on January 7th, after a one month and half fasting; an abstinence from eating meat and dairy products, fasting mornings to noon or 3:00 pm and more devotions to the Christian doctrines.

The spicy smells of food, mainly the hot rich red-coloured chicken stew which we commonly call keey wot, had the power to waft all the way to the church upstairs much like incense, and I started to feel hungry. My heart was still preoccupied with the aroma that could easily impregnate one's clothes like a 'Paris' perfume, as Ethiopians would like to describe. The same friends who welcomed me and my wife to our new life in Canada, were sharing this most sacred of meals with us at the church. After about four months, I started to get used to the new form of Injera bread and all the spices accompanying it here in Edmonton.

Ethiopia celebrates three national holidays in September. Much like the Western Christmas and New Year. And dining at this time of the year happens both indoors and outdoors. In the southern part of the country, particularly the Gurage Communities (one of the ethnicities in Ethiopia) prepare themselves for almost a year for a holiday like Maskal (the finding of the Genuine Cross) which falls towards the end of September. At that time, women, mostly the Gurages, work hard on making Kocho, one of the most popular foods in the Southern part of Ethiopia. Kocho is another traditional flatbread made with enset fruit, or 'false banana' due to similarities between the two fruits. It takes months to prepare, squeezing its thick flesh into a dough-like mass, wrapping it in large green leaves, burying it in the ground. It takes months for the buried Kocho to get fermented and the process of shaping it into flat loaves before it is baked and served: another painstaking task that women in this part of the country perform.

Other most common foods include beyaynetu, a vast array of prismatic vegetables, curries, salads, and other kaleidoscopic stews and lamb cut in strips, tiibs, a pan-fried dish with butter, garlic, and onion, among other ingredients. Doro Wot is an Ethiopian curry version made of mainly chicken drumsticks or wings. What makes it so special is that it is cooked and served in a hot sauce of butter, onion, chilli, cardamom, and berbere. It could be also served with hard boiled eggs. The other famous Ethiopian food, Tire Siga includes a cube of red raw meat served with Injera, and a very spicy sauce.

My Ethiopian farewell ceremony included many of these dishes. I didn't have to have a dog's nose to smell the festive, glowing wind that continuously wafted from the highly decorated Mesobs, traditional cylindrical table with cubical cover on top to place a huge plate for many dinners. And of course, the beguiling kitchen on that memorable night almost coinciding with the eve of the Ethiopian new year. As I arrived in Edmonton, the taste of kitfo was at the back of my mind as I poured my non-stop musings onto my friends and wife here in Edmonton.

"Bemote! Bemote!" (On My Dead Body!), people beg you as they attempt to feed you. This Ethiopian culinary/dining tradition is known as gursha. It entails feeding another person by placing, with one's hand, the bowl or a bite of spicy food with Injera gently in the mouth of the other. It is indeed an intimate act of friendship or love, and a tradition that most lovers practice in Ethiopia. This habit defies every and all norms in the West around personal space and hygiene. Imagine how hard it could be to practice now in the era of COVID-19. Yes, I am overwhelmed with nostalgia, knowing that it will be a long while before I am able to return to my homeland. Mellowness envelops me as I enjoy tella, traditional Ethiopian beer and tej, a rich honey wine.

The day after my arrival the heavy Ethiopian breakfast and the first coffee ceremony awoke me to yet another chapter in life in Edmonton. Firfir was the suitable meal for breakfast after the welcoming night! One of the heavy Ethiopian breakfast meals. It is a saucy, spicy and oily food mixed with the basic—Injera. There is no ingredient left out when making firfir. Imagine onions, vegetable oil or butter, garlic paste, tomatoes, dried beef or simply minced meat, salt, palm-sized pieces of Injera, all compacted in a pot. It takes up to half an hour of cooking; for a lazy cook like myself, up to an hour, and that's why it is preferable to have it for breakfast, on weekends or your days off. The only special breakfast comparable to firfir is genfo, a modest yet likeable porridge made by adding dry-roasted barley flour to boiling water and stirring the concoction with a wooden utensil until it develops a smooth, yet extremely thick consistency. The porridge is then transferred to a bowl, and a hole is created in the centre, usually by using a finjal (a small-sized coffee cup). This well is filled with clarified spiced butter and berbere. Genfo is often shared and consumed by pulling the thick porridge pieces from the outside and dipping them into the spice blend in the centre. Unless paired with your strong coffee, you find yourself in bed again in less than an hour.

"Coffee is ready," my wife announced as I headed to the window to explore my new home, contemplating the past and the future: standing at the juncture. Long before meeting members from our community in Edmonton, long before having my two kids, long before I explored the food courts and coffee shops in the city, I used to sit for hours partaking in bunna maflat, the Ethiopian coffee ceremony as we call it there; it literally means "to brew coffee". The ceremony itself looks like a ritualized form of making and drinking coffee in households. The loose grass and flowers spread on the floor upon which the ceremony takes place, and the inviting aroma of incense makes the house so special and adorable. The very purpose of such an event is to get together with relatives and neighbours and discuss pressing social and political matters. During the ceremony, there are a minimum of three rounds of coffee creating a general feeling of relaxation, chatting about political, social, religious, and economic ideas, to the point of exhaustion.

Once my wife got back to her routines, I began to develop a walking habit, exploring my new hometown. I was so happy to see some Sabian or Ethiopian inscriptions on the walls and commercial houses of the neighbourhood. Around Edmonton's busy 107th Avenue, mainly between 97th and 124th Streets I would hear—and still do—Amharic, Tigrigna, and Oromo languages, Ethiopian and Eritrean common languages spoken by many people. Like back home, these streets are filled with all that the Habesha [Abissinian] Ethiopian and Eritrean communities need. Besides the convenience stores, barber shops, butcher, and hair salons, there are restaurants I only rarely visit.

When no one was around, during the early moments of my settling in town, I used to call back home too often. With only a $5.00 calling card you could talk with families and friends forever. I spent hours talking to my friends and relatives back home, especially the powerhouse of information, my sister Woini in Addis Ababa, my first ever call back home.

"What are you up to?" I do not tell her that I am now at City Centre Mall food court in Edmonton for my half-hour break. My wife is so angry at me for having forgotten my lunch box in my rush to work.

"Just finished my four-hour duty and I am on lunch break, getting back to duty in half an hour."

"You should be in a very comfortable zone. Lucky are those who are in North America," my sister said.

"You think so? That is not the reality. I wish you could come and see. I used to think that way, but I am starting to feel that life is totally different."

"How so?"

"You remember that two stanza poem made by a bored Ethiopian immigrant in North America?"

"No. What was it?"

> America Binor Yedelagn mesloshal,
> Hode Behamberger Tewetiroshal.

> You thought I am in North America living a real dream,
> Alas! My hamburger stuffed belly looks like nothing but a drum.

It has been years now. I am more Canadianized. I haven't gone back since I left my country. Memories from back home including food are fading little by little. I don't mind eating what I use to call 'fake Injera.' With the hustle and bustle of life and with the kids around and my wife being busy, even this Injera becomes a luxury at times. Sometimes I grab the double extra-large coffee with the egg and cheese sandwich. Egg sandwiches are the safest, as eating bacon contradicts my religious belief.

Challenges are great avenues for self-improvement. I have gradually started learning to cook. As my wife tells me now, I am an expert in firfir. It takes me over an hour but I also recently mastered Shiro too, a dish primarily made of powdered chickpeas or broad beans. It is to be prepared solely with water and salt or with additional ingredients like minced onions, garlic, ground ginger, tomatoes, and chilli-peppers. I know I will not therefore die of starvation here. KFC and McDonald's are a little bit heavy for me as I am more of a vegetarian due to our long Orthodox fasting seasons. Vegetarian Indian dishes like Chana Dal and Chana Masala are my favourite ones nowadays, and I eat them comfortably when I fail to pack my lunch or dinner to work. The Chapati can't replace Injera but it is not that bad on days when food is scarce. Though still picky, as a world citizen, I tend to taste every food. The rice with some vegetables from the Chinese restaurant at the food court at City Centre Mall is still one of my favourite foods, since it agrees with my finicky nature.

Against all these odds, my Ethiopian food and other traditions still persist. It even looks like it is passing on to the new generations in a foreign land. My little daughter, who is now only four, said, "I like Injera Beateta." She meant Injera with the hot meat spice. My son, who turned six recently, likes tiibs. Of course, Ethiopian dishes now blend in with more standard Canadian meals. It is hard to drive by McDonald's as they insist to have a Happy Meal, but at least they have something to love and talk about from our ancestral cuisine. They always start their meals praying: "Besimeab

Wowold Womenfes Kidus Ahadu Amlak" (In the Name of the Father, the Son and the Holy Spirit; One God Amen) and "Temegen Getaye!" (Thank God), when they are done with their meal, and they adore the word Ameseginalehu (Thank You!).

Food Ties

Leilei Chen

Grandma is here visiting me.

    I felt her presence when I cracked the egg into the batter as I was making pan-fried cake for breakfast. Grandma passed away in 2004, the same year I moved to Canada. In Edmonton's cold, snowy, dark mornings, making breakfast alone in the kitchen, I thought of Grandma making green onion pancakes over the beehive coal stove in our home in Suzhou (宿州). I was a sickly child then and unusually picky about food. To coax me into eating more, Grandma boiled dumplings, each only one-third of its normal size—one perfect bite for my little mouth. Or, she made me green onion pancakes. In the 1970s, when every family was poor in China, she would even sandwich an expensive egg into the pancakes for me and my sister.

    Grandma, I am here, "overseas" as you would say, craving your green onion pancake.

    What an exquisite process she had. First, she made a dough. Then, sprinkling in chopped green onions, she kneaded the dough into a multilayered paste. She lined the iron wok with soya bean oil and pan-fried the paste. The best part was seeing her lift a few layers of the paste with a pair of chopsticks just when the other side turned gold and carefully pour an egg in. She turned the paste over. A few minutes later when the egg was cooked, she moved the pancake on a plate, round and golden like the moon falling from the sky. It smelled like comfort. And the first bite filled my mouth with crispy flakes followed by soft, tender, nestled egg. The flavour imprinted on my finicky taste buds ever since.

When father called me from the other side of the Pacific Ocean telling me Grandma passed away, I was loaded with my work toward an English PhD and a family trying to settle in Edmonton. I didn't even have time to fly back to Anhui for her funeral. Since then I often felt her presence beside me, watching me making breakfast in my Edmonton home on those dark mornings.

I was a frantically busy grad student and needed a simpler technique. Omitting the paste-making process, I simply stirred flour, water, green onion, and egg all together, poured the batter into a grapeseed-oiled pan, and fried it until both sides turned golden. The flavour was similar although the texture degraded from a rich sensory diversity to a singular softness. Waffle-like, just a bit smoother, chewier. The less-refined process made the cake less satisfying, the texture not nearly as rich.

Sarah, my daughter, loved it anyway. She always took the leftover batter cake to work and ate it for lunch or as a snack in her office. Unlike when she was in elementary and junior high school, she no longer felt ashamed eating homemade Chinese food in public spaces. I drove her to the LRT station one day. She vividly recalled her feelings of confusion and guilt when she was in grade five eating the green onion pancake at lunch. "Yuck, what are you eating?" Her peer's question screamed more xenophobic repulsion than genuine curiosity. For a long time she only brought cold sandwiches to school. Tasteless, she now told me, and yet she pretended to eat as happily as other kids.

I grew up with Grandma. My parents were artists working for a local opera troupe and were often away from home for a long, long time giving performances. In those leisurely afternoons, Grandma often welcomed the neighbours to have afternoon tea at our home. Being part of the social circle, I often got the question from our guests: "Leilei, what do you want to do when you grow up?" Grandma always answered for me, "Go abroad and study overseas!" She beamed with confidence and hope.

I couldn't help but think my grandmother had something to do with my move. She might not have been serious, but her repeated response seemed to express her good faith in overseas learning, which perhaps implanted the seeds of aspiration in me when I was a little girl, which later grew into a reality.
"Grandma, going overseas is a hard journey!" I knew she knew. I could see Grandma smiling. She was proud that I had done it. Grandma was born in 1919, the year when the May Fourth Movement happened. This was a time when China was going through a stage of transition from a feudalistic to a modern society, a time when China opened its door to the outside world, hungering for new ideas and technologies from the West. She was one of those women who was lucky not to have crippled, bound feet. "My feet were wrapped tightly with a long, long cloth, four smaller toes bent under my front soles. I was not like other girls who accepted this as Fate. I always, always unbound my feet in the evening. It just hurt too much!" Grandma was illiterate, but she liked to tell us stories and showed us how rebellious and free-spirited she was.

Grandma always drank jasmine tea. She liked the fragrance. When she poured hot water from the thermos into her teacup, the jasmine tea floated on the surface. She put the lid back on, letting her tea brew for a while. Then she uncovered the cup, smelled the sweetness. The tea leaves had fallen down to the bottom. The white little jasmine flowers remained floating on the surface, delicate-looking. Such a delightful sight. She gently blew them away and had a sip.

Grandma would have enjoyed entertaining her guests from my inkstone tea tray. In my homecoming trip to Guangzhou in 2011, I was amazed to see this artifact. The tray was carved out of natural inkstone, the unique type called lü duan yan (绿端砚) only found in Zhaoqing (肇庆). Unlike most types that were black, mine was green with touches of other pigments here and there that ranged from light yellow to brown and to pitch black. Integrating these dots and lines and brushes of colours harmoniously, the tea tray became a sculpture of a peaceful scene of nature—a serene lake; a little thatched house on the lakeside; a flight of stairs leading to the house; the rising slope of the mountain; sprouts of pine trees surrounding the house, standing on a boulder, perching over a cliff, hiding and waving from behind the mountain top; a spectacular full moon on top.[1] It was such an old-fashioned thing. Yet I couldn't resist its charm and mailed all 118 pounds of it back to Edmonton.

    I sat in front of the tea table beside my kitchen. Pu'er tea (普洱茶) contained digestive nutrients. A perfect choice after eating Grandma's green onion pancake. The miniature Buddha statue sitting on the right side of the inkstone tea tray greeted me with his usual carefree big smile. The three-legged toad and pixiu (貔貅), two Chinese legendary creatures that would bring good fortune, sat on the other side. In between the Buddha and pixiu were five piglets in a row, symbolizing luck, status, longevity, wealth, and joy. These were tea pets made out of zisha (紫砂), or red earth. The first cup of tea would always go to them, a ritual that expressed respect for one's subordinates. I poured Pu'er tea over my tea pets one by one. Their mouths emitted bubbles as if they were giggling. What a beautiful chorus of laughter on this tea tray stage! These little creatures certainly enjoyed tea and its social life. Grandma would have loved to be part of the tea ceremony.

    The hardest part of going overseas was not to use a foreign language or get used to a new way of life but to constantly process people's assumptions. Life felt like swimming upstream. My literary theory professor assumed that I was well versed in Marxism. Of course, I came from a so-called Communist country, but wasn't Marxism a German thing that anyone from any Communist country would need to study in order to know well? Didn't Marxist theory mutate to suit the Chinese context as a result of the Communist power? I was surprised at such an assumption—ashamed, really. I didn't know very much about Marxism, honestly. There had been a token unit on it in an undergraduate course I—an English major—had never really studied. But I was too confused to explain this to the professor on the spot.

    Food was a soothing balm after those thorny moments. My husband, Guang, and I liked bringing pork belly stew to potluck parties. It was called hong shao rou (红烧肉) in Mandarin: our favourite dish and one Guang took pride in cooking so well. Better than any one of its kind we had ever had in any restaurant. Including the Michelin star restaurants. With a few lines of vegetable oil in the wok, Guang stir-fried ginger, green onion, and garlic until he smelled the chorus of their aroma. Then, he poured the pork belly cubes in and stirred the ingredients together for another little while. Afterwards, he added soybean sauce, oyster sauce, sugar, dried red pepper, star anise, and stirred a little more. Feeling ready, he poured in water and stopped just when it immersed everything in the wok. He covered it with the lid. When the stew started boiling, he turned down the heat to low and let it simmer for an hour or even longer. When all the juice in the wok was absorbed by the pork cubes, the dish was ready to serve. I couldn't help tasting a piece. "Ummh, I am in heaven." Sarah always said so when eating Dad's hong shao rou. Sometimes, we only used pork in the stew. On many occasions, we added other ingredients at different times to enhance the flavour and enrich the nutrients: fried tofu, dried long beans (干豆角), dried bamboo roots (笋干), dry salted fish (咸鱼), or various kinds of fresh vegetables such as cauliflower, seaweed, potato, cabbage, pumpkin, or taro root. Pork belly stew was Grandma's favourite dish, too.

    I never knew we could be so creative with food until we started our life in Canada. Depending who were our guests, we reinvented pork belly stew in multiple ways. For our friends coming from northern China, we made the stew a bit saltier and added more spices to it. If we had guests from Shanghai, Ningbo, or Suzhou (苏州), we enhanced the sweet flavour. Almost all our local Edmontonian friends and those from elsewhere around the globe loved whichever way we cooked it: the pork belly stew pot was always empty at the end of the parties.

    Grandma would be happy to see me using food to build my overseas home. In our circle of friends, Guang enjoyed his reputation of being the best cook. When he wasn't loaded with work, one of his greatest pleasures was to cook for the dinner parties we hosted. Seeing people enjoy the food he cooked gave him great joy. Guang said, "food is universal. No matter who you are and where you are from, you always need food. Food is the best way to connect with people, to introduce your culture, and to learn a new culture." So, through the tie of food, we were connected to people from all walks of life in our new home.

The coronavirus pandemic broke such connections all of a sudden. Social gatherings were restricted all over the world to prevent the plague from spreading fast. We no longer had parties. Cooking now became a pastime to spice up the monotony of home confinement. I was as busy as ever, but finally I had more time for cooking.

I decided to make Grandma's multilayered green onion pancake for our breakfast. The exquisite kind with an egg in the middle. The pancake had nurtured me before. It would occupy my mind and keep me sane now. I would share it on WeChat and Facebook. In the picture, Grandma's pancake lay on the plate, golden and round like the full moon falling from the sky.

NOTES

1 See also the description of this tea culture element in my short memoir piece in "Life Begins at Forty" in Julie C. Robinson, ed. *Looking Back, Moving Forward*. Toronto: Mawenzi House. 2018. p. 181.

Culinary Arts

Wendy McGrath (*Canada*)
Sauerkraut Tableau and Other Art Installations

Luciana Erregue-Sacchi (*Argentina*)
Pen Portraits with Mate and Asado

Sauerkraut Tableau and Other Art Installations

Wendy McGrath

Sauerkraut: a Still Life

Once, when I was a teenager, my grandmother had a crock full of sauerkraut fermenting in the dining room of her house. There on a chair in the corner, hand-shredded green cabbage was weighed down by a smooth, heavy rock on top of a white china plate. Where my grandmother got the rock, I don't know. I didn't ask at the time, just accepted this prop as a necessary component of the sauerkraut tableau. Thinking of this now, the rock in the kitchen seems puzzling to me. It was winter, and the ground was covered in snow. How long had she kept the rock in anticipation of this installation?

I remember I took a black and white photograph of her checking the sauerkraut's progress. She was wearing a printed cotton dress (she rarely wore trousers) and was bent over the crock intent on her creation.

My grandmother's sauerkraut making was a lengthy process of transformation. When she cooked, when she baked, she took simple tools and ingredients, manipulated them and elevated them to high art. My grandmother's kitchen was, in a way, her studio space. This was where she transformed the everyday into something transcendent. The light brown colour of the crock, the white of the china plate, the smooth grey rock—a still life assembled.

That photograph I snapped of my grandmother is long-lost. The still life she created in the corner of her dining room has disappeared. What is left to me, however, is this image of my grandmother as an artist as she assembled disparate, everyday components and transformed them into something wonderful.

Pflaume kleisl

My grandmother made an unusual soup for my father once, maybe twice when I was growing up. Those were the only times I ever saw or tasted this rare creation. My grandmother said it was plum soup and told me its name in German. What I remember hearing her call it was: pflaume kleisl. It was a sweet soup with prunes, raisins, and little dumplings. Pflaume kleisl could be eaten hot or cold.

It was a cloudy, dreary, grey-looking concoction that made me think of stones, rain, and mud. A Bruegel painting given to my father in a large mason jar. It was treated like some magical elixir, but I couldn't understand why this was such a delicacy for my grandmother and my father. I thought it tasted horrible, especially cold. Who eats cold soup? I never asked my grandmother for the recipe.

As an adult, I thought I might give the mythical pflaume kleisl another chance. If it was such a delicacy, it must have had something going for it, something I might have missed as a child. My tastes might have changed. And I did remember liking the looks of the little dumplings in the broth. I don't speak German so trying to find a recipe was a bit of a challenge. First, I Googled the basic ingredients of what I remembered:

> German sweet soup with prunes raisins and dumplings

I got some hits for recipes for similar soups from other parts of Scandinavia and Eastern Europe. I couldn't be sure it was the soup my grandmother had made. I turned to Google Translate, English to German: Plum = Pflaume

Wiktionary says a colloquial meaning for pflaume is vulva. Maybe a reference to the dumplings' sculptural shape? Certainly no one ever made reference to that connection when I was a kid. Soup imitating a female nude? Not in this house! My grandmother always seemed the serious sort, but I do remember my grandfather telling some story of how my grandmother had once laughed to the point of hyperventilation over a joke involving a bee and a penis.

Had my grandmother found humour in a bit of innuendo over the name of a plum? If she had, not only had I misunderstood the unique taste of this soup, I'd missed the joke my grandmother might have smiled to herself about as she spooned this moody-looking mixture into a mason jar.

To tease out the meaning of kleisl, the soupy second word in the name of this dish my grandmother made, I again turned to Google Translate. Kleisl translates as "small". Did I have the spelling correct? Simply switching around the two middle vowels in the word changes the meaning. Kliesl translates as "dizzy". What if I add an "e" to kliesl? This simple addition of an "e" turns kliesl into kliesle: which translates as "pee". This bit of bathroom humour, especially paired with the colloquial definition of pflaume I encountered, couldn't possibly be related to the precious soup my grandmother made.

I choose to settle on pflaume kleisl: little plum?

Deciding to make my own version of pflaume kleisl, I source a couple of possible recipes online. Prunes, raisins, sugar, cinnamon stick, vinegar, perhaps orange and lemon, and tapioca to thicken the mixture. I cover the dried fruit with water and set it to boil. Stir in sugar, vinegar, tapioca, and cinnamon stick and turn my attention to making the little dumplings. I source a dumpling recipe online. A simple mixture of eggs, flour, water, a pinch of salt. As I stir, the dough becomes a stiff, golden substance. Like putty. I scoop up small spoonsful of the dumpling dough, scrape from the spoon and dumplings fall away into the bubbling broth like miniature sculptures with beautiful, unpredictable shapes. They do look like vulvae. This has turned into a most erotic soup...

And the broth is more a golden, beautiful amber than the dull grey I remembered from childhood. More Rembrandt than Bruegel. I taste. It is delicious. I am surprised and strangely happy. I have discovered or, rather, rediscovered a dish, a taste from my childhood that has transformed from ugly to beautiful. The taste memory has changed for the better. I have painted over what I remember as the old Bruegel broth with a palette more befitting a Rembrandt, it seems.

Making this soup became a stirring in of questions unasked, recipes unwritten, meanings undefined. Pflaume kleisl became an overpainting of taste and memory by some simple little dumplings, prunes, and raisins.

Springerle

I run my palm over the surface of the lino block—grey, hard, and smooth. It waits for the event that will mark the beginning of its life. This event is not a first breath taken in, nor a broken shell hatching out. Whatever this print is to become will begin with a cut, a gouge: a digging into its flat shell.

I am making linocut prints at home. I use my dining room table and my kitchen counter for a workspace and the line between the processes of creating art and food blurs. I place my paper over an inked linocut and run a rolling pin over it. I use a kitchen spatula to spread ink on an old Tupperware plastic pie rolling sheet. What was once a kitchen and dining room is now my printmaking studio.

My hands want to return to familiar patterns—flowers, geometric shapes. These patterns are part of my genetic memories; memories I draw upon literally and figuratively; memories that are an embossing and debossing of details and tastes and impressions. As I make the first cut into a lino-block, it triggers a flash-image: Myself as a small child. In my grandmother's basement suite kitchen not that far from the basement suite my own family lives in. Opening the cutlery drawer in my grandmother's kitchen.

Shyly resting among the knives and forks are beautiful little wooden blocks with shapes carved into them. So remarkably different from the everyday utensils, different from anything I've ever seen in my grandmother's kitchen. These shapes are inside a carved grid of four squares. I remember: simple stars, cross-hatches, flowers. My grandmother must tell me they are molds for special cookies. Springerle. Then my memory shifts to another place, another time. A scene in my aunt's kitchen, on her farm in Saskatchewan.

My grandmother is there too, and she and my aunt are making these cookies. Very special cookies. Springerle means "little jumpers". My aunt's kitchen smells of licorice and as they roll the dough and cut the shapes, I propel myself down the staircase that leads from the kitchen to the bedrooms on the second story of the house. I bump down every stair—a little jumper. The scent of licorice and talking, licorice and laughing. I go up and down the stairs. My grandmother and aunt have cut out the Springerle, which line cookie sheets on the kitchen table.

> *Can I taste one?*
> *No, they must rest before they're baked.*

I knew how much I hated to rest, to be forced to take a nap in the middle of the day. As soon as my aunt's and grandmother's attention waivers from these beautiful little carvings, I sneak a taste of the unbaked dough, a corner off one of the precious cookies. Ugh. How could such beautiful things taste so awful? Can I trust this taste-memory from so long ago? As I create linocuts in my kitchen, I decide to explore this suddenly-made connection between printmaking and baking. I was excited to merge the processes of printmaking and baking to create/re-create the Springerle I remember—or misremember.

I gather ingredients: eggs, confectioner's sugar, flour, hirschhornsalz (baking ammonia), anise oil, anise seeds. The scent of the anise oil is like Christmas, birthdays, and every happy moment in one tiny bottle. I have managed to find a Springerle rolling pin and I run my palm over its surface. Simple shapes of birds, stars, flowers, fish, leaves, and geometric shapes are cut into it. It is itself a work of art.

The eggs must be beaten until they are like spun gold. I use my small electric hand mixer. Add the sugar. Flour. The mixer dies for its efforts. I mix the dough by hand. The feel of the dough, the scent is from some distant childhood moment. I shape the pale dough into a flat, thick disk and put it to rest in the fridge. The Springerle dough waits for the event that will bring it to life.

The next day I take the Springerle dough from the fridge. I

press the rolling pin into and over the dough, slowly embossing and, at the same time, debossing little shapes. I watch these shapes emerge in miniature: fish, a bird, a rabbit, those "little jumpers" appear from a matrix of yielding dough. There is the same sense of anticipation and wonder in watching these shapes emerge from nothing as there is when I pull a print. Baking and printmaking: making Springerle is art and artful.

My childhood second-hand experience became the matrix for the prints I would create as an adult, at home, in my kitchen.

I have just created a small editioned series of flower prints on my kitchen table. They are drying on the coffee table in my living room. At the same time, the Springerle cookies I created dry in a large glass jar in my basement.

Food as Art

Right now, there are several food-art tableaus in my house. I revel in their simple, honest beauty. The commitment needed to create art, and to create beautiful food is the same. Often, tools, techniques, and sensitive perception of what you need to gather to create something transcendent are also the same in art and food.

I feel satisfied having plumbed my childhood, searched for recipes from my childhood that first made me aware of the artistic possibilities all around me that I can continue to reimagine, revisit, and redefine my memories to write, create art, and make beautiful food.

Art and food take time and, right now, I have all the time in the world.

Luciana Erregue-Sacchi
Pen Portraits with Mate and Asado

Portrait of Past Mate[1] Drinkers:

River Plate, 1537

"All Spaniards, men and women, and all Indians, drink these dusts in hot water," one dismayed Jesuit priest wrote, lamenting, "And when they don't have the wherewithal to buy it, they give away their underpants and their blankets... When they stop drinking it, they fade away and say they cannot live." Fading away, faded, my memories of drinking mate back home, in Argentina, at university, keeping me alert for exams. After their 1537 entrance, the Spaniards acquired the habit of drinking mate from the Indigenous population of Paraguay. In the course of a few decades they expanded the use of yerba throughout the southern part of their empire, from Potosí to Santiago de Chile to Buenos Aires.

1830

Thomas Carlyle visits Paraguay and of his encounter with Dictator Francia, he describes in *Miscellanies* how "In exercise of the primitive and simple hospitality common in the country, I was invited to sit down under the corridor, and to take a cigar and mate (cup of Paraguay tea). A celestial globe, a large telescope and a theodolite were under the little portico; and I immediately inferred that the personage before me was no other than Dr. Francia."

1834
Argentinian Dictator Juan Manuel de Rosas, a contemporary of Francia and Carlyle, would always have a servant by his side, ready to pour him mate. He would drink the Paraguayan beverage all day, and "Whenever he wished, he would stretch his arm, would take a few mate sips, to return it to his servant right after."[2]

Portrait of Two Girls Discovering Mate:

Argentina, 1973
The white and black granite floors feel cold on my sprawled legs. My knees are wrinkled and dark from so much playing on dirt roads. Other familiar limbs, covered in green and orange opaque hosiery move back and forth, spinning, gliding their stacked heeled pumps in white, turquoise, yellow. Their square toes threaten to kick the kettle my friend Mariana and I are jealously guarding. I am the designated cebadora, a five-year-old, making sure the water spills in the centre of the mate gourd, filled three quarters with yerba, and one quarter with sugar, the mate plant sticks floating in the cold water. Nobody keeps an eye on our sugar intake. The volume of conversation increases, as does the smoking.

It is always about "El Viejo" returning from Spain...former President Juan Domingo Perón is the person on everybody's lips. Mariana and I muffle the adult laughs and arguments with the insistent slurp from the mate. Its bombilla or metal straw whistling to us when enough is enough. We are mastering the first commandment of mate drinking...the same person must always pour the water: "La Cebadora" for the most part, a female. Mariana and I take turns drinking, slurping, pouring the water until the kettle empties. Clacking heels, departing sounds, farewells, sighs, cackles, final sips of whisky "on the rocks," the stomping of cigarette butts, signal the party is over. The trail of yerba spreads all around us spilling over its container, a wooden box with an engraved gaucho riding a horse on the lid. Tonight, Saturday, June 19th, 1973 the family agrees to return the next day for Sunday lunch, our tradition. I have yet to learn that mate means the actual plant, the ceremony, the container, and the best way for friendships to grow if someone invites you over for a round of mate or "matear".

Portrait of a Dictator Drinking Mate:

Puerta de Hierro, Spain, March, 1973
   His life slowly unfolds, there are no commitments, no schedules. He rises very early and has a light lunch prepared by his Spanish cook, Rosario. She met General Juan Domingo Perón in 1960, when she was a maid in a hotel in Torremolinos. The General had been on a pilgrimage of sorts, seeking asylum in the Caribbean since his deposing in 1955 in Argentina at the hands of the military-led Revolución Libertadora. Argentina jumps from tyrannies to dictatorships, the way it has always been, a tradition much like drinking mate. Rosario followed the General to Madrid once Spanish Dictator Francisco Franco authorized him to settle there indefinitely. After the meal Rosario hears the General gargling, getting ready for his siesta. He claims this way he enjoys two mornings in one day.
   In 1973, the General still amuses himself chasing the ducks in the park of his Puerta de Hierro house, on Navalmanzano Street, catching up with visitors or writing one of his many articles on exile, and the Latin American situation that newspapers from all over the globe commission him. In the early evening he heads to the kitchen to drink mate with Rosario. His eighteen-year pilgrimage begins to show on his demeanour. His backcombed hair and knowing smile, however, still remind his people of eternally young tango singer Carlos Gardel.
   Argentinian men worship at the feet of tangueros and Perón relishes in wearing his many masks: benevolent leader, tanguero, thug, glamorous figure. He glances towards the garden, dressed in his immaculately pressed pants, smelling of Atkinsons' Lavender cologne, his military training evident in his formal yet relaxed stance. Rosario offers the General the mate gourd, brought from Argentina

by one of his acolytes; she pours hot water from the kettle on the stove. Perón slurps from the silver straw as his unruly eyebrows point towards the checkered floors. The General's body devours his own legend and—shortly—will be devoured. "El Viejo" sips the mate, he grunts, he stammers, opening a tiny rift, a moment of delay within the urgency of his return allowing the hot, bitter drink to wash away that other bitterness, exile, widowhood. Will he embrace or reject the left-wing youth factions who clamour for his leadership, or will he side with the extreme right groups of his party? The greenish liquid descends through his body, warming, and alerting him of the challenges ahead. He thinks of Argentina, in the middle of winter right now, and of his long dead wife, Eva, her embalmed lips even colder than Buenos Aires in July. His new wife, hotblooded former bar dancer Isabel, frets in the living room, over her tailleur with her couturier, interrupting the General's mate induced trance. The house is otherwise silent, waiting for the other shoe to drop. Drinking mate means he is back home. Almost.

Portrait of a Father Preparing Asado:

Brandsen, Argentina, Sunday, June 20th, 1973
I do not know what my father thinks of Fathers' Day. For nearly twenty years he has been fatherless. He has the dad body to go with it. My grandmother always tells us stories of shopping for clothes for my father in the gorditos—chubby section—at the high-end department store. Feeding all those around him is his highest calling in life. My father arrives at my aunt Emmy's house, the epicentre of our extended family life, full of boisterous women and silent men, loud boys and quiet girls. The house has a special room for asados, Argentinian barbeques: el quincho, or hut, a common fixture at the back of the newly built social housing developments dotting the countryside during the 70s.

My aunt's husband, a car mechanic obsessed with car racing and fishing, volunteers to pick my father up. The Sunday ritual of becoming a criollo begins. Our mom and we wave my father goodbye. He leaves the house already sweaty from the effort of carting into the trunk of the Ford Falcon, the essential elements of asado: the wood to light the fire, the boxes of tinto—red—wine, and the meat, each serving following the standard serving of a pound of beef per person. There are chorizo sausages spiced up with pimentón and oregano, there is vacío: striploin—lomo: sirloin—and costillar: short ribs. He brings along his own chimichurri sauce, made with ají molido, garlic, oregano, parsley, and oil to sprinkle like a love spell on the meat as it grills. Argentina's culinary tradition, a blend of creolized European and Arabic preparations mirrors the way in which European foods and identities were transformed during the first half of the twentieth century. Its mainstay is a beef-based diet.

    Traditionally, men cook the beef ribs outdoors on an open fire or a grill. The asador, surrounded by his friends or male relatives, would discuss the sharpness of their gaucho knives, their handles usually in bone or silver, with engravings of thistles, like the ones dotting the Scottish countryside. The facón dagger became a partner of the legendary semi-nomad rider of the Pampas, his survival tool, and ultimate virility symbol. My father's knife is of modest size, its blade almost reduced to a sliver, due to so much sharpening against a slab of grey stone he keeps at home.

    My father pours some Cynar aperitif in his stocky glass, and reads *Clarín*, one of our national newspapers. In large letterings, the headline "VUELVE PERÓN: MASSIVE CROWD DECAMPS AT EZEIZA AIRPORT TO WELCOME PERONIST LEADER": the old man's return bringing him right back to the matter at hand. He sharpens his gaucho knife, wisely sprinkling coarse salt with his chubby, agile fingers on the meat spread out in organized rows on the butcher's block. In twentieth-century Argentina to be a criollo is either romanticized and idealized or considered backward and interfering with "progress".

    As a middle manager at the Provincial Government in the city of La Plata, my father's carefully planned weekend asados allow him to keep progress at bay, re-asserting his rural masculinity and his position as head of the household at large. Years later, I realize that the solitary moment of asado preparations are my father's way to cope with the pressure life throws at men from his generation during these violent years. Like all Argentinian males from the 70s, his role is that of asador in much the same way a woman's role is that of cebadora de mate. Argentinian asado is the one and only meal typically prepared by a man, routinely invoked by Argentinian men as a definingly manly activity. Such an act necessitates the feminization of women in the creole-criollo Argentinian culinary complex which explains why it is mostly a woman's role to pour—cebar—Argentina's national beverage, mate.

Portrait of Young Leftists Lighting a Fire:

As my family sits to enjoy my father's asado, two of my uncles, Quico, a bearded theatre director and intellectual whose parents escaped the misery of the Spanish Civil War, and Carlitos, a baby-faced, blue-eyed hippie, a well-off radio and nightlife pioneer from my town, are foregoing today's asado to head to the Ezeiza airport to welcome the General. Carrying nothing more than their jean jackets and their wallets, they hitchhike alongside other compañeros, part of the Southern column of left-wing sympathizers, and some of them outright guerrillas. As they advance next to the Bridge Number 12 by the Ezeiza Airport, their column starts singing about openly declaring war on the right-wing group of the Peronist party they all belong to. People breathe the imminent violence in the air. Perón's advisors order the plane to land at the nearby Morón Airport anticipating what may happen once their leader touches down. My father sits last at the main end of the adult table, closest to the grill, and enjoys an especially juicy piece, as he oversees, like a God, how his flock is reacting to his offerings. He reminds me of the benevolent General Perón. But do not tell him; he detests the guy.

After the asado, my father heads with a family friend to play cards at a nearby rural village; meanwhile, closest to the stage where Perón is supposed to address the crowd, the right-wing faction of the party occupies strategic positions from where to control—and eventually shoot—the leftist columns. At around 2:00 pm, people hear the first sounds of gunshots. My uncles begin to run as far away from the scene by crawling close to the ground, the way Quico's father, a socialist veteran from the Spanish Civil War, ran away from the Franco forces assailing his town. By 3:20 pm, all is blood and chaos. A car is engulfed in flames; this is no asado. As my uncles make their way back to our town, the lunch hour extends well past 3:00 pm. Our family is away from the TV; we have no clue of what is happening to my uncles.

It is 4:00 pm and as the embers on the parrilla die down, so do my aunts' voices, who now inside the house cannot believe what they see on TV. All is confusion, young men running in different directions, Molotov bombs thrown towards the running crowds, cars ramming against running youth, ponchos flying. People are confused. "It is the communists," says one youth. The sound of ambulances overlaps with gunshots, people abandon the site however they can, some filling a truck to the brim, shouting "Perón! Perón!" Some crawling. Our family keeps vigil, eating the leftover salads and the chopped cold meat from the asado, served this time on butcher blocks and eaten as finger food. I just smell the remnants of the fire.

Portrait of a General Eating Asado:

Argentina, October 8th, 1973

It is Monday. Exactly at 11:20 am, the Olivos residence opens its doors. President General Perón is in a jovial mood. He has received gifts of gold and silver, yet he is playing with a plastic toy, a gift from a Tierra del Fuego law maker. He is keen to talk to the youth assembled there. There are young up-and-coming politicians who cannot believe their fortune of standing next to their leader. The culinary ceremony of asado reproduces itself across millions of other Argentinian households. The General, now president, celebrates his seventy-eighth birthday. He is frail, near death. Only he knows how very close to the end he is. Everybody around him pretends he is the same caudillo from thirty years ago.

At noon he takes part in an asado party for 5,000 military officers. The officers gift Perón a sword that belonged to José de San Martín, the father of Argentinian independence. He beams and enters history. After his death, the country will not see a return to democracy for twelve more years. The delicate equilibrium between private and public, has forever been shattered, and curfews on gatherings mean asados are smaller affairs. The voices, other times cackling and loud, are now mysterious, somber, whispering names of people who I will never see again. Soon other meanings associated to the word asado become part of those whispers.

Portrait of a Country Digesting Asado:

Buenos Aires, May, 2017
In her essay "The Art and Horror of the Argentine Asado", Argentinian writer Mariana Enríquez explains that asado and political violence are inseparable in the history of the country. Enríquez refers to the 1976-1983 dictatorship and how the connotations of asado permeated the paramilitary activities because the illegally detained were tied and tortured with a 220-volt electrical probe called picana onto a table splattered with water, the burning flesh, due to electrocution as if the body had been "cooked" like beef on a parrilla or grill.

At the end of 2012, almost thirty years after the return of democracy, the government organized an asado at the former Navy Mechanics School (ESMA), the main clandestine detention centre where almost 5,000 people were held captive and tortured during Argentina's last dictatorship. The event was highly polarizing. While a sector of the political and cultural establishment deemed it an instance of collective digestion of grief, as researcher Cecilia Sosa affirms, others saw a betrayal to the memory of those who perished or were tortured at the centre.

The ghosts of General Perón, and the Ezeiza massacre remain buried beneath the ashes. My family's asados became a rarity after 1983, the return of the country to democracy. It was as if those weekly criollo celebrations were an emotional crutch softening the blow of the transition between youth to maturity for my father and the other men of the family.

Portrait of an Argentinian Missing Mate:

Edmonton, May, 2020
My taste buds do not care that I am writing about mate from my snowy Canadian outpost. They are craving the release of all that is bitter about life right now, the whole lockdown, the "new normal".

In the best of cases there is never enough critical mass for me to start a mate round. Imagine now, when we cannot pass the gourd and straw around. The virus has upended this practice also back home. I always pondered about how anti-hygienic the practice of sharing the straw was. We Argentinians stubbornly kept doing it in our offices, in concerts, in family reunions, with friends, in the park: our dirty little secret. On the upside, women in my country now have one fewer chore.

I long to pass the gourd around; the murmur; the noise of the heated water trickling through to the bottom filled with green powder; the anticipation of the warm metal straw resting on the tongue, hugged by the lips, the slow sucking-in motion; the aspiration of the warm—and now moss-green—liquid. I miss the action returning the gourd to the cebadora, erasing in that gesture all the minute instances of difference, replacing coldness with warmth and friendship, repeating this choreography until everyone in the round has satiated their craving. I miss saying, "gracias" once the rush has subsided after my four or five mate rounds. Gracias means, "please stop passing the gourd to me. I am done." The cebadora will get offended if you say "gracias" right after the first mate. Delayed gratitude, concentrated, valued, handed over.

Notes

1   (MAH-teh)

2   José Arturo Scotto, *Las Diabluras del Tirano Juan Manuel de Rosas* (Buenos Aires: Biblioteca Histórica, 1896), 183.

About the Authors

Yasser Abdellatif

is a writer and poet from Cairo, Egypt. He has lived and worked in Edmonton since 2010. He has published four fiction books, two poetry collections, and translated many literary works from French and English into Arabic. He writes mainly in Arabic although his works have been translated into English, French, German, Italian, and Spanish. He has participated in literary events and festivals in France, Spain, Colombia, Germany, Netherlands, Malta, and United Arab Emirates. Abdellatif was a resident of the International Writing Program (IWP) at the University of Iowa in 2009. His debut novel, *Law of Inheritance* (2002), won the Sawiris Prize in 2005 in the young writers' category. His collection of short stories, *Jonah in the Belly of the Whale*, won the same prize in the category of prominent writers in 2011.

Mila Bongco-Philipzig

was born in Manila, Philippines and arrived in Edmonton in 1984 with a grant for graduate studies at the University of Alberta. After completing her master's, she moved to Germany on a scholarship towards a PhD. In Munich, she met her husband and they have one son. Mila and her family have lived in various places around the globe, preferring to be on the road experiencing various cultures and perspectives rather than being tied down with a mortgage. This changed in 2007 when they decided to call Edmonton home in order to provide a more predictable environment for their son, and to enable him to form long-term friendships. Mila works at Stantec and is active in the community. In 2016, she published two bilingual children's books (Pilipino and English), both reflecting her interests in family, travel, multiculturalism, and diversity.

Leilei Chen

Dr. Leilei Chen is a scholar, writer, and literary translator. She wrote Re-orienting China: Travel Writing and Cross-cultural Understanding (University of Regina Press, 2016) and translated Steven Grosby's *Nationalism: A Very Short Introduction* (Oxford University Press) into Chinese (Yilin Press, 2017). Her memoir/travel writing, essays, and poetry translations appear in *Home: Stories Connecting Us All* (2017) and *Looking Back, Moving Forward* (Mawenzi House, Toronto, 2019), *The Polyglot, Literary Review of Canada, Women of China, The Chinese Journal*, and *Latitude 53*. She teaches at the University of Alberta.

Luciana Erregue-Sacchi

is a Canadian-Argentinian art historian, writer, and editor. Her poetry and creative non-fiction essays have appeared in the anthologies *Looking Back, Moving Forward* (Mawenzi House, 2018), *Relatos Entrecruzados* (Editorial Mapalé, 2020), and in blogs and literary magazines worldwide. Luciana guest edited *The Polyglot* magazine's ekphrastic issue, "CanLit: Curating our Canons" (Spring 2018). In 2019, Luciana was the Edmonton Arts Council Artist in Residence, and was selected as part of the Literary Arts cohort at the Banff Centre. Luciana writes on her blog, SpectatorCurator, about her life as an art historian. This volume is her first endeavour as part of her activism, for diversity in Canadian publishing, *Laberinto Press*.

About the Authors

Shimelis Gebremichael moved to Canada about four years ago. Shimelis is originally from Ethiopia where he practiced journalism in both print and electronic mediums. He is a Master of Arts in Communications and Technology (MACT) graduate at the University of Alberta. He also did his MA in Journalism and Communications and BA in Foreign Language and Literature (majoring in English) at Addis Ababa University, Ethiopia. Over the last four years, he has volunteered for CJSR, Centre for Family Literacy, and his church in Edmonton. He is passionate about making a difference in the community through his literary works (poems, prose, and other forms). He also aspires to continue his journalism career in both English and Amharic languages. Shimelis is married and blessed with two beautiful kids.

Tazeen Hasan In addition to maintaining her own blog, Tazeen regularly contributes hard news, investigative pieces, and editorials on topics ranging from science and technology to geopolitics and entertainment for a variety of online and print news outlets. For several years, she contributed travel and history pieces to Asharq-al-Awsat group of newspapers in the Middle East, and Jang and Nawa-e-Waqt groups in Pakistan. She has traveled extensively in the Middle East, Western Europe, parts of South Asia, Africa, and North America with a focus on exploring history and culture. She is fluent in both written and spoken English and Urdu, with a working knowledge of Arabic, Punjabi, and Hindi. In 2020, Tazeen completed her studies of Journalism at Harvard University Extension School.

Wendy McGrath is a writer and artist who works in multiple genres. Her poetry/photography collaboration with Danny Miles, drummer for July Talk and Tongue Helmet, is trying to find a home. McGrath's most recent spoken word project, BEFORE WE KNEW is her second CD with Sascha Liebrand. Her first project with Liebrand, *BOX*, is an adaptation of her eponymous long poem with the group Quarto & Sound. "MOVEMENT 1" from the CD was nominated for a 2018 City of Edmonton Music Award in the Jazz Recording of the Year category. McGrath continues her artistic practice in visual art—including printmaking and artist's books.

Marco Melfi is an Edmonton poet whose work has been published in *The Prairie Journal*, *FreeFall*, the Edmonton Poetry Festival's *Poetry Route* and *40 Below: Volume 2*. His chapbook, *In Between Trains*, was published in 2014, and Marco was the recipient of the Sharon Drummond Chapbook Prize.

Peter Midgley is a poet and storyteller born in South Africa and based in Edmonton. He has performed in several countries around the world and has published three children's books, one of which, *Thuli's Mattress*, won the International Board on Books for Young People Award for Literacy Promotion and has been translated into twenty-seven languages. His latest poetry collection, *Let Us Not Think of Them As Barbarians* was released in 2019 (NeWest Press).

About the Authors

Adriana Oniță
    is a Romanian-Canadian poet, founder of *The Polyglot*, a multilingual magazine of poetry and art. She writes poetry in English, Spanish, Romanian, French, and Italian. Her passion for languages has led her to pursue a PhD in second language education. She is the author of the ekphrastic chapbook *Conjugated Light* (Glass Buffalo, 2019). She is a recipient of a Killam Scholarship and is a PhD candidate in Educational Policy with the University of Alberta.

Ana Ruiz Aguirre
    is a Cuban-Canadian cultural researcher and development strategist. Born in Santiago de Cuba and currently based in amiskwaciwâskahikan (Edmonton, AB), her work focuses on the development of cultural equity through research, writing, and curating.

Maitham Salman
    was born in Iraq and came to Canada in 1998 as a political refugee. He has published a novel, *Husks as Big as My Country*, and a collection of short stories, *The Dirhams of Caliphate*, in Arabic, as well as many articles and short stories in Arabic and Canadian newspapers and magazines.

Asma Sayed
    is Canada Research Chair in South Asian Literary and Cultural Studies at Kwantlen Polytechnic University. She is a multilingual writer, translator, and academic originally from India. She holds a PhD in Comparative Literature from the University of Alberta, and writes regularly on issues of social justice in literature, film, and media. Her publications include five books and numerous essays, fiction, creative non-fiction, and translations in periodicals, anthologies, and academic journals. In 2016-17, she was one of the authors selected for Edmonton's Borderlines Writers Circle hosted by the Writers' Guild of Alberta.

Anna Marie Sewell
    specializes in collaborative multi-genre projects. MacEwan University's 2019 Writer-in-Residence, her creative process draws on heritage (Mi'gmaq/Anishinaabe/Polish), music, and multiple languages. Edmonton's fourth Poet Laureate, she's published two poetry books. Her first novel, *Humane*, arrives in 2020 from Stonehouse Press. Her bread recipe was published in 2019, in the University of Alberta cookbook *Our Stories, Our Food*. Her online home is prairiepomes.com.

Acknowledgements

We would like to acknowledge that the concretion of this project would not have been possible without direct financial support from the Edmonton Arts Council through their Cultural Diversity in the Arts Grant. We also would like to recognize the Writers' Guild of Alberta, since most of the contributors in this anthology took part in the WGA Borderlines Writers Circle, an initiative that naturalized the co-existence of local and immigrant writers in the wider Edmonton literary community. Lastly, I would like to acknowledge the invaluable contributions of Kimmy Beach, Alicia Chantal, and Matthew James Weigel, and all of those individuals who directly or indirectly made this project possible. You know who you are.